Shameless:

Unleash Your Message, Impact & Power

Charisse Sisou

visibility maven to
women here to change the world

Original and modified cover art by Wonderlane and CoverDesignStudio.com,
redesigned and made glorious by Rosanne Romiglio of CleanClearCreative.com.

Cover photo by Michael Wilson of StagePhotographic.com

ISBN: 069207757X
ISBN-13: 978-0692077573 (Charisse Sisou)

Dedication

Dedicated to shameless, maverick women everywhere:
Entrepreneurs, mothers, CEOs, coaches, executive directors, speakers, board members, business owners, executives, nonprofit founders, authors, mentors, professionals, and any other purpose-driven modern-day queens, courtesans and witches here to break the mold and shift the planet. (*You know who you are*).

Contents

Introduction:

She lights the way

The dance of the woman who leads

Women trill their joy, their ululating darting from open throats like silken plumage tossed over the slow military march of the drums—*DOUM che-keh chek-chek, doum chek-chek... DOUM che-keh chek-chek, doum chek-chek...* The distinctive rhythm announces the approach of a wedding procession wending its way down the street, long before the *zeffah al'arusah* comes into view.

In a tradition upheld to this day by some Egyptian families, the bride-to-be leaves her childhood home, journeying on foot to the new home she's to share with husband and family. The maiden is accompanied by a large party of musicians and family and community members.

The *zeffah* is purposely loud and raucous, the noise calling people out of house and field to spill along street or lean out of window, adding their cries and claps to the cacophony. It is a very public rite of passage for the young bride-to-be.

Until the *zeffah*, the maiden has lived a relatively sheltered, private existence, rarely experiencing mixed company outside immediate family. Suddenly, she is the focal point of a crowd of family and strangers alike—an acute focus laced with the leering, teasing knowledge of what awaits her that night in the marital bed.

I imagine the bride, head bowed beneath her veil, flushing red under the heat of all those eyes trained on her as a young woman on the brink of sexual awakening.

And herein lies a dilemma: *the bride-to-be leaves her family home a girl, but cannot remain so as she heads into her wedding night.*

Embedded within this tradition is another woman, whose role traces an ancient thread running from hand to hand, from grandmother to mother. An incarnation of womanly magic and intelligence, of embodied feminine leadership: the dancer.

The dancer immediately precedes the maiden. Her womanly hips sway and shimmy while her head floats level, the better to balance a great candelabra crown, the *shamadan,* ablaze with rows of candles.

Her grounded presence serves as a shield for the girl. The dancer is accustomed to being in the public eye, and handles the arrows of scrutiny, judgment and energy that accompany high visibility with aplomb.

In fact, the dancer deliberately provokes attention with her fiery headdress and frank sensuality. *She is deeply and unapologetically feminine*.

By virtue of the dancer's presence, the maiden is transformed. Though she left her home a girl, the bride arrives at her new home a woman.

This is how I see the modern-day woman who leads: businessowner, warrior, CEO, goddess, entrepreneur, priestess, executive, mother, midwife, maverick, crone. She is a crucible of transformation, through her very body.

You, my love, are the Dancer.

It is through your unabashed, unapologetic, *shameless* presence—hips swaying, head held high—

That you cut through the noise and are SEEN...

That you transmute intensity with compassion, vulnerability, tender self-care and emotional virtuosity...

That you make your most grounded, creative, intuitive business decisions, accelerating your results and expanding your impact...

That you commit and show up, even when your hair is on fire—*especially* when your hair is on fire!

It is your full, voluptuous presence that attracts clients, followers, team members, volunteers, donors, readers, audience, stakeholders, and partners—those you most desire to serve, *those you are here, on purpose, to serve.*

You are the dancer, paving and lighting the way for the girls who quietly watch your every move to see how it's done—*to see how women lead*. You inspire other women to take up more space and share their gifts. Your presence disarms men, inviting them to embrace their own *yin,* moon, or Feminine aspects. All learn from you—your unabashed presence changes everything.

Every woman has untapped resources of wisdom, healing and guidance in her body. When we learn to trust our cellular intelligence, release shame and reclaim all parts of ourselves (including the juicy bits!), we become magnetic... *unstoppable*. Able to show up as all of who we are, bringing clarity and power to our messaging.

In this book, *we step into full presence:* uncovering where shame is holding us back or dimming our light, and embracing our shadow so we may truly shine.[1]

---

[1] I first heard the story and history of *zeffat al'arusah* as told by one of my mentors, the brilliant author, dancer, researcher and dance ethnologist Sahra Kent (Sahra Saeeda), in her *Journey Through Egypt* certification course. Any embellishments, flights of imagination and inaccuracies are all mine.

You cannot, you cannot use someone else's fire. You can only use your own. And in order to do that, you must first be willing to believe that you have it.

—Audre Lorde

1

This book is for you if…

Telltale signs that you're hiding in plain sight

Raise your hand if any of the following apply to you:

You want to have greater impact, and reach more people with your message.

You want to raise awareness or shed more light on a cause near and dear to your heart.

You have a big purpose. Maybe even global-big.

You want to be noticed and appreciated for what you do.

You want to be paid what you're worth.

You want to be a sought-after speaker and thought leader.

You want to be taken seriously.

And yet…

You don't feel clear about your message.

You are on the brink of a brand refresh or full-out rebrand.

You are adding a new product, program or service and don't know how to align it with the rest of what you do.

You've worked with copywriters in the past but haven't been satisfied with their work—because they don't "get" you or your voice.

Or, have any of the following happened to you:

When hearing of a service you offer or what you did for a client, the response you get is: "I didn't know you did that."

When being introduced, your colleague says: "This is my friend. She is... does..." then turning to you, says, *"What do you do again?"*

When talking to a potential referral partner, they confess: "I don't know how to explain what you do." (This is the kiss of death.)

You've been passed over for the role you've been vying for. *Again.*

Your potential client says no... then yes to a competitor.

You are amazing at what you do, and yet it's "feast or famine." You struggle to have a steady, consistent stream of business.

The idea of networking, or public speaking, scares the bejeezus out of you.

Or, you're networking and speaking, but not getting the ROI (return on investment) you want from either—while watching colleagues' businesses steadily grow as they follow similar paths.

A competitor with (frankly) half your talent, skill and experience is attracting more clients—and making better revenue—than you.

You're referred to as the "best-kept secret" in your industry.

Everyone knows who you are (by face, or name)—but no one knows what you do.

That last one was my flavor-of-choice. *I was hiding in plain sight*.

I was one of the most visible, longtime members of a business community, hundreds—even thousands—of people strong. Many people knew who I was—by some compelling thing I had said from stage, seeing me dance at a dance party (as a former professional bellydancer, I'm hard to miss), or we'd hugged, exchanged business cards, or shared a conversation.

Everyone knew who I was. *No one could tell you what I did*.

I was brilliant at showing up. But when it came to stating clearly what I do or for whom, not so much. I'd captivate the room and then... mic drop. It was like I was playing an unintentional game with my ideal client: "Wanna work with me? Gotta catch me fiiiirrrrsssssttttt!" (voice fades as I take off running in the opposite direction). Often, I left them without even a simple call to action or way to connect with me.

I call that "fake-out" visibility. Visible insofar as going through the motions, but unseen in all the aspects that would help people take action on my ideas. It hurt my business, badly.

Invisibility wasn't doing my cash flow any favors, but it felt *safer*. Until the day I found myself asking, "How has playing safe worked for me so far?"

Playing safe had allowed me to stay comfortably small. Under the radar. Less vulnerable. Rocking no boats in the immediate vicinity. As if covered by Harry Potter's invisibility cloak, I could escape danger with impunity—strolling under the noses of people who may judge, dislike, or hurt me without being detected.

The only problem was that I also hid myself from the people who might love, champion or, you know, *hire* me.

So, what does the opposite look like? With high visibility, clear message, magnetic brand?

When I first started attending bellydance shows, I would watch the other dancers in wonder. What made certain ones stand out? It sometimes had to do with skill—but that wasn't it entirely, because the audience could be as captivated by the master dancer as the beginner, rocking the three steps she knew.

"It" had to do with the dancer's presence. Her sheer confidence and comfort in her own skin. Her showing up entirely as herself, with passion, whole-heartedness—whole-*bodied*-ness—in her dance.

I had many of these fully embodied moments in my dance career—and others, too, where I lost the feeling, caught up in insecurity, or seeking approval. But in my very first performance, that I write about in my chapter in *Courageous Hearts*[2], I nailed it:

---

[2] Joy, Linda, et al. *Courageous Hearts: Soul-Nourishing Stories to Inspire You to Embrace Your Fears and Follow Your Dreams.* Inspired Living Publishing, 2017.

I was so present... I was a vessel, and the music danced me. *The crowd and the cells of my body cheered. My joy had found me. I had found my joy. There was no going back.*

Being seen requires standing in one's truth—in every inch of the body, in every word of one's story—so profoundly and unapologetically that, like a lightning rod, we attract the people with whom we're contracted to work, live and play, from client to life partner.

ꙮ ꙮ

A quick note on using this book:

Throughout, I reference action steps, research, associated links and additional resources. **You can find everything and more on the Book Resources page at:**

ShamelessMovement.com/book resources

So, you don't have to worry about typing in those long pesky URLs to check out a source or video yourself. It's all on the Book Resources page. *You're welcome!*

ACTION STEP: *Time to self-assess.*

Is shame secretly running the show behind your marketing, and your business? On a scale from 1 to 5, score where you tend to fall in the following scenarios. Put the number next to each of these lines.

And, this goes without saying, but: *Be honest.* Don't answer the way you think is "right," but the way that is true for you, in this moment. A great "hack" to doing this, precede each statement with, "If I were to be totally honest..."

(Would you rather print out this exercise? Find the worksheet and PDFs of all action steps at ShamelessMovement.com/bookresources).

① ⑤

When I have the opportunity, I...

___ Take up less space..Play big

___ Hide my opinion.......................................Reveal my true thoughts

___ Mask my emotions..Share my emotions

___ Avoid being in the public eye.................................Show up openly

___ Undercharge.......................................Charge above-market prices

___ Discount my prices..Stand firm on pricing

___ Hide...Choose to be more visible

In general, I...

___ Am a perfectionist..Embrace my flaws

___ Don't like my body..................................Love and accept my body

___ Am depressed..Am generally happy

___ Constantly explain actions.........................Act without explanation

___ Apologize constantly..Act without apology

___ Work all the time...................Spend equal time at rest as at work

___ Compare myself to others..................Celebrate others' successes

___ Overfill calendar with social activity......Revel in some alone time

___ Walk on eggshells..Breathe easy

___ Need to constantly prove myself...............Have nothing to prove

When I make decisions, I typically...

___ Maintain the status quo...Shake things up

___ Avoid an unwanted outcome.....................Lean into what I desire

___ Have few choices..Have many choices

___ Overcommit...Balance my schedule

___ Am afraid to fail...Take failing in stride

Add an extra point each for the following:

___ I have a website.

___ I feel proud of my website and feel that it represents me well.

___ My photo is somewhere on my website.

___ My photo is on the home page of my website.

___ A video of me is somewhere on my website.

___ A video of me is on the homepage.

___ The About page includes something about me, the founder.

___ I have an "About the Founder" page on my website.

___ My bio includes more than credentials and accomplishments.

___ In my bio or on my website I talk about my big *why*.[3]

___ I have shared the personal story behind my work.

___ I have appeared on social media in video. (Add a point for every platform in which you've posted video featuring your lovely face: YouTube, Facebook, Instagram, LinkedIn)

___ I've appeared in a live video stream, online.

___ My LinkedIn profile is in the first person.

---

[3] For more on the power of why, see Simon Sinek's talk, *Start with why—how great leaders inspire action* at ShamelessMovement.com/bookresources.

___ I am in a networking group. (Add a point for every different networking group you're in, currently.)

___ I regularly speak in public. (Presentations, talks, what have you.)

___ I have an "elevator speech."

___ I blog regularly.

___ I post on social media regularly.

___ I have a mailing list.

___ I communicate with my mailing list regularly.

Total up your numbers. This is your Visibility Quotient, or VQ:

22 – 50: Under-a-Rock Maiden

My dearest darling, please know that there is no judgment in this house. You are where every High-Visibility Queen starts—and to where we all occasionally want to return! (You know, that moment when you're in line at Panera and think, *I could be that barista... How easy and fun would that be; just show up, get paid. Who needs this marketing stuff, anyway?*)

Know that you are safe. Key for you will be taking baby steps out of your comfort zone, so you don't go running back to your cozy hideaway more than occasionally.

51 – 80: Hiding-in-Plain-Sight Maverick

Ah, you trickster goddess, you! You luscious tease! (I mean that in the best sense of the word.) You reveal, then cover, then reveal, then cover... I feel you, sister. This is where I struggled in my business for far too long, underpaid, undermarketed and underwhelmed by my results. The seeds are there, so key for you is looking at what's working for you... and doing more of it.

81 – 110: On-the-Verge Goddess

Gorgeous, you are so close! You have many pieces in place, and now it's about going deeper, perhaps being more vulnerable than you've ever dared before. (I give specific guidance on this in a later chapter). What is the still-niggling fear? Where is the new place of resistance? What is the thing you know you need to do, that's been on your list of marketing strategies to implement for ages, that you keep putting off... ? (Oh, can we all relate.) That may be the very ticket to your High Visibility Queendom.

Just like when you're on the yoga mat, feeling for the delicious edge of a pose that stretches your muscles, without crossing over into anything forced or painful: Press your edge, mama. *Press your edge.*

111 – 135+: High-Visibility Queen

Go on with your awesome self! At your high level of visibility, vulnerability and doing "all of the things," this book will be about refining and amplifying your efforts. About leaving no stone unturned in terms of your own resistance to expansion.

As a sorceress of visibility, you know there is always room for improvement, always that next big exposure that will take you to the next level—speaking live to your biggest audience yet, getting on the coveted stage of the premier event of your industry, hosting your own television show, or being featured in a high profile interview, say, with Oprah... The sky is the limit for you, precious one.

Check in, deep. What is your next expansion... and what next step will take you in that direction?

The higher the number (out of a possible 135+), the more comfortable you are in the spotlight—or, I should say, the more willing you are to step through the discomfort to be seen. (I've been on stages since I was 4 years old and I still get nervous and my mouth goes dry every time I stand up to speak in public.)

That said, in truth, we dance between all the stages—some days rocking out as High-Vi Queen and the next, wanting to crawl back Under a Rock (Maiden). It is an ongoing dance that is, by the way, completely normal.

Were you surprised by your results? How much are you hiding, without realizing you're hiding?

Gut check: It doesn't matter how "visible" we appear from the outside, if inwardly we feel disconnected from or misaligned with our public persona. (*Will the real me please stand up?)*

Are you ready to draw a line in the sand? No more hiding! Email me your results at shamelessauthor@gmail.com, with "No more hiding" in the subject line. I'd love to hear about what came up for you: what did you see, what did you notice, what did you get?

EXTRA CREDIT: ***Journal it out.***

As a lifelong writer and professional copywriter, I'm a big believer in the power of words to transform. Words are a part of how we process through things, as women. (My best friend and I joke about the "boy version" of a story where we "get to the point" faster—sometimes we just have time for that—versus the girl version, where we meander, reveling in the truth that *the story is the point.*

Use a journal to take notes, do the written exercises in this book, and reflect on the body activities. Journaling by hand, on paper, will deepen and accelerate the process.

SISTERHOOD AMPLIFICATION: ***Sisterhood amplifies growth.***

With the "Action Step" at the end of each chapter, I'll include a "Sisterhood Amplification." Women need sisterhood like we need oxygen. It sustains us, fuels us, spurs us higher.

(Hint: Sisterhood Amplifications are great for Book Club group discussion points or activities! *Just sayin'*.)

For this exercise, do this assessment with a friend and share your responses. Or if you're in a women's business networking group or mastermind, go through this book together. Need more copies? Get them at ShamelessMovement.com/book. (Go ahead, get more *Shameless*. ;))

And hey, don't leave *this* sister out—*I* want to hear all about what you learn together. If you are reading this book with a women's network or group, let's meet up online! For a live Q&A and discussion with the author, email me at shamelessauthor@gmail.com with "Author Q&A" in the subject line. It would be my absolute pleasure to connect with you.

The more of us willing to take a stand for who we are and what we do, without shame... the better. I am here to take a stand with you.

ℰ𝒪 𝒞𝒬

I am a Woman
Phenomenally.
Phenomenal Woman,
that's me.

— Maya Angelou

2

Why Shameless?

A note on the title

There are two sides to my use of the word *shameless*.

First, marketing often feels pretty "shameless" for women, and not in a good way.

To brag about our unique brilliance, to boast about what sets us apart from the rest of the marketplace and industry; to name ourselves a leader in our field, to "shamelessly" pursue our ideal client or supporter or donor; to boldly state our worth goes against the grain of everything we're taught growing up.

And yet, that's exactly what we MUST do in order to connect with our peeps:

Market ourselves, *shamelessly*. Clearly state our value, what we bring to the table, what problems we solve, why we're different, and who we serve, unequivocally.

Girls, in general, are not encouraged to crow about their accomplishments, their beauty, or their mad skills. And I'm not talking ancient history, here.

Popular teen band One Direction released the hit *What makes you beautiful* in 2011, featuring these lyrics:

"You're insecure...
The way you smile at the ground it ain't hard to tell...
You don't know you're beautiful...
And that's what makes you beautiful."

How many of us have heard at one time or another:

Have you no shame?
Don't brag.
Don't boast.
Who do you think you are?
You don't want people not to like you...

If you did agree with a compliment, or respond with pride to recognition, you may have heard:

Well, isn't somebody *getting too big for her britches!*
You don't want to get a big head.
Aren't you *full of yourself?*
Self-absorbed, much?

This attitude is so engrained in our culture, you may have caught *yourself* thinking along these lines when you've given a woman a compliment—only to have her surprise you by agreeing with you! (No judgment here, I just want you to get a sense of what we're up against, societally speaking).[4]

---

[4] There have been some humorous and disturbing explorations of this topic: the Buzzfeed video, *When a woman takes a compliment*; Zooey Deschanel's hilarious response as the character Jessica Day in *New Girl*, when she unexpectedly receives a compliment; or the firestorm of response to the Twitter post, "Piss a man off today. Tell him you agree with his compliment of you." Find these links on the Book Resources page at ShamelessMovement.com.

We may have "come a long way, baby" from earlier generations of women who couldn't own land, get educated, or work outside the home. (Heck, US women have only been able to *vote* since 1920, after suffragettes, jailed and beaten, fought for the right—finally granted the same year the Miss America pageant began. *Go figure*.)

Then add to the mix significant layers of underlying messages we receive as women via religion, race, ethnicity, class, sexual orientation, etc.; from within our communities and mainstream culture.

One of my clients reported not wanting to speak up and share her dissenting opinion in a work meeting because she didn't want to be labeled as an "angry Black woman."

Another chafes under the overwhelming assumption of heterosexuality in everything from networking events to speaking engagements, and hides the fact that she's a lesbian.

Still another hid an integral part of her methodology, her "secret sauce," because she thought people would think that being spiritual and a channel would make her too "woo" or New-Agey (which she most definitively is *not*), and refuse to hire her to coach them on business.

(What she learned is that *her* clients *love* that she is a fourth-generation witch, and a powerful one at that. If heads of state could consult with her grandmother on election results, couldn't a CEO benefit from the same caliber of advice?)

The harsh truth is that... *Brace yourself...* Not everyone will like you. Painful, I know. But seriously, this is a big deal for most of us, myself included.

Your message will not align with everyone. And that's okay. *In fact, it's kind of the point*. (Let that sink in.)

I'll speak more to the power of specificity and the importance of your unique story when we talk about pinpointing and speaking to your ideal client in chapter 9, *Clarify Your Desire*.

We have internalized messages that encourage us to downplay our value and hide our true stories. Until we acknowledge these limiting beliefs, they act insidiously behind the scenes, secretly sabotaging our best marketing efforts—and silencing our message before it's had a chance to reach the people who need it most.

Having journeyed this path myself, and witnessed my clients come again and again to the branding table burdened with this invisible backpack of gremlins, I developed a system that *tackles* these internalized messages. This approach reprograms you for visibility by embracing some of the very characteristics you've been taught to hide, as the foundation of your strength, brilliance and success as a woman leader.

I'll unpack that system in chapters 6 through 10.

So, to sum up this chapter so far: the messages we received growing up and to this day discourage us from promoting ourselves, because to do so is *shameless*, which is *"bad."*

Got it? Good. Now hold on to your panties, because *this goes way deeper.*

Every leader, but especially women, can relate to feeling pressure to turn DOWN the volume on who they are—their capabilities, radiance, sexiness (*especially* sexiness), emotionality, sensitivity, vulnerability, beauty, pride, even literal speaking volume—to make someone else feel comfortable, whether in a business, corporate or even personal setting.

How many times have you sat on your hands...

Bitten your tongue...

Held back feelings—tears, rage, even laughter—because you didn't want to be judged for being "too" emotional, "too" sensitive, "too" *too...*

How many times have you made yourself smaller without realizing it? Conceded a valuable boundary, to make someone else more comfortable? Taken up less space?

Now, let me be clear: *You are no timid mouse.*

I was on the phone the other day with a gentleman who didn't know that much about my business, which weaves women's empowerment with messaging strategy, and body with business (because, in my experience, they are all inexorably intertwined.)

He made a leap, "So, you help insecure women to be more confident?"

I sighed. I felt irritated, but gave him the benefit of the doubt. We do live in a *Lean In* culture that actively penalizes women for being women, then reprimands them in the next breath for not doing or being *more*. Patriarchy... *what patriarchy?* I quickly corrected him.

I explained that I work with leaders who, by and large, are incredibly accomplished, powerful women who have already made waves in their business, nonprofit, market or industry. That it's less about confidence or insecurity—and more about having hit a wall, or plateaued, without understanding why, because they're "doing everything right." It's about getting into even greater alignment. About massively increasing impact. "Their branding and copy have been working... up to a point," I said. *"And now they're ready to be even more of who they already are."*

This is not training for the faint of heart. (Is it ever?)

This is about stepping into the fullest expression of your leadership as one of the many women who are being called at this point in time and history, to bring the planet back into balance.

You are a woman with purpose. A big, audacious purpose. Multiple passions and purposes. *And the truth is, it isn't even about you.* This process of expansion, widening and deepening your impact, has everything to do with the people you are here to serve. *The people who, up until now, couldn't find you.*

And the tools that you have been given have taken you as far as they can. The tools you need now, to do your greatest work yet, are tools that have been long-buried. The work in this book—getting "shameless"—is all about accessing those tools.

The thing is, we, as women, are freaking BRILLIANT at adapting and putting up a flawless front. We have learned how to go through the motions, say the right things, put the pieces in place, *follow the rules*...

We have developed sneaky Jedi-mind-trick ways of holding back parts of ourselves that others have found threatening while *looking* like we're "out there" boldly marketing, and "have it all together."

I have a long and colorful history of being a total NINJA at hiding in plain sight. Of justifying why I stayed small, or continued to get less than optimal results. Of playing it safe. Of carefully avoiding stepping on any toes.

Which is why I felt compelled to write this book and share, step-by-step, how I overcame—continue to overcome, because this is an ongoing process—my disempowering stories, narratives and beliefs. To stand in the light of ALL that I am. *Without shame*.

Which leads me to the other side of *Shameless*...

ACTION STEP: *Receive compliments fully*.

Receiving compliments with grace sends a message to the cells of your body every time you do it: *Yes, I am worthy. Yes, I am enough*. New habits of thought replace old.

Resist the urge to brush off the compliment ("What, this old thing? I got it on sale!") or boomerang it back ("Thanks—ooh, and I love how your hair looks today!" or "Thanks, but I wish I had your figure!")

No "buts" allowed!

Just say thank you... then stop talking. Make kind eye contact, say "Thank you," and leave it at that. When you first try doing this, you'll notice what amazing feats of willpower it takes to do this simple act! Sit in the discomfort... it will pass, I promise!

Or, say "Thank you, it's true!" This is one of my personal favorite responses, and the one I encourage my clients and audiences to adopt. "Thank you, it's true!" I say it with such delight that I usually end up getting a laugh—and everyone feels good. (Because the dark side of refusing to receive compliments is that it feels really *ugh* to the compliment giver. Don't believe me? Try complimenting someone who won't receive it. It's like handing someone a gift they won't accept. It takes all the fun out of the giving of it.)

Another of my favorite responses, if you want to spread a little love when receiving a compliment from another woman, you can also say "Thank you," then PAUSE—because nope, you are not allowed to sneakily turn this into a boomerang; let the compliment fully sink in—then say, "Takes one to know one." *Wink.*

SISTERHOOD AMPLIFICATION: *Compliment in circle.*

Turn up the volume on this exercise by doing it in circle with women. The next time you're with your sisters, or your book club, or having dinner with a group of girlfriends, go around the circle and practice complimenting each other and *fully receiving* the compliments, with grace.

Notice and embrace the squirminess; it's okay, it's all a part of the process. This is new, uncomfortable territory. Be brave and take a stand when you see one of your sisters try to shrink back, or start talking in circles. It is okay—no judgment here, and: gently remind her that this is about *accepting* compliments, remember?

Or try this Praise Shower variation:

When I trained for my *Dancing for Birth* certification, so I could teach pregnant women how to dance through labor, we took turns standing in the middle of a circle. As you stood there, the rest of the ladies in the class would circle around and deluge you with compliments. They'd come in fast, heavy and loud from every direction.

Just shut your eyes, turn palms out in a gesture of openness, and *take it in*. It feels awesome, like an embodiment of the James Taylor song, "Shower the People." *Shower the people you love with love.*

ஐ ஐ

Owning our story can be hard but not nearly as difficult as spending our lives running from it. Only when we are brave enough to explore the darkness will we discover the infinite power of our light.

— Brené Brown

3

What's shame got to do with it?

Or, thank you, Brené Brown

Why *do* we play small?

Why do we as women downplay our strengths, appease our offenders and abusers, stand by and watch as other women get trashed, and hide in plain sight—say, for example, have a whole website for our business where not a single image or word talks about the founder (who just happens to be the woman whose vision drives the whole enterprise).

Why do we confuse the market, so they don't know what we do or how clients work with us?

Why do we refuse to get specific about who we serve, niche down, narrowly define our clientele?

And any of the other ways that we DON'T market in a way that's authentic, compelling and irresistible to the people we're meant to serve...

Why do we hide? And how do we stop?

I'll dive deeper into the why's and how's later, but in a nutshell: We hide because *we don't feel good enough*. We undercharge because *we don't feel worthy*. We mask our imperfections because we conflate perfection and lovability.

All of these messages come from shame. (Now you know where this is heading, so this is your last chance to drop this book and run screaming for the hills, or back into that comfy closet!)

It is largely thanks to Brené Brown's runaway TED talk on vulnerability and her research on shame that we can broach this subject with some familiarity. Even so, it's a difficult topic for folks to face, head on. (For instance, people often invite Brown to speak to their groups... about anything *but* shame and vulnerability.)

Everyone has shame; few want to admit to it.

And although we wantonly toss the word *vulnerability* around, few are truly, boldly, vulnerable—especially in their marketing and copy. After all, marketing and the words we use to reach clients and talk about our business are our "public persona." And vulnerability feels like weakness. It feels scary. We're not quite sure what to share and what not to share. (Not to worry, I offer guidelines on exactly how to use the power of vulnerability, and gauge how much is too much in chapter 10 on sharing your story.)

But before I jump into how shame interacts with your marketing and shadows your copy, let's get on the same page about these terms.

Caution: Before you go thumbing off to the next chapter, like "hey, yeah, I watched the TED talk." Slow down, *chicacita*. Resist the urge to skip this part, with an "I know this already." That phrase is one of the sneakiest ways our inner gremlins keep us from growing.

So, what do I mean by shame? One way to approach it is to understand what it's *not.* Shame is not guilt. From Brené Brown's TED talk on shame:

> *Shame is a focus on self, guilt is a focus on behavior. Shame is, "I am bad." Guilt is, "I did something bad." ... Guilt: I'm sorry. I made a mistake. Shame: I'm sorry. I* am *a mistake.*[5]

For many of us as we were growing up, there was not much distinction made between *doing* something bad, and *being* bad.

Brown defines shame in this way:

> *Shame is the intensely painful feeling or experience of believing we are flawed and therefore unworthy of acceptance and belonging. Women often experience shame when they are entangled in a web of layered, conflicting and competing social-community expectations. Shame leaves women feeling trapped, powerless and isolated.*[6]

How might closely held beliefs around feeling unworthy impact how we talk about ourselves, our businesses and our causes? How might shame be hijacking the driver's seat in our messaging and copy?

Don't get me wrong; men experience shame too. A telltale sign for men that shame is secretly running the show is a "flip-switch" around certain subjects: he's either shut down, or pissed off.

For women, however, there is a layer that doesn't exist for men: *We are shamed for the very skin we're in.*

Every woman shares this pivotal moment—the first time she realized that her body was treated differently, was somehow *wrong,*

---

[5] Brown, Brené. *Listening to shame.* If the title of this chapter and leading quote give no indication, I am a huge fan of Brown's work. See this video and others, as well as recommended readings on the Book Resources page at ShamelessMovement.com.

[6] Tucker, Judith Stadtman, "Motherhood, shame and society: An interview with Brené Brown, Ph.D., author of *Women & Shame*." *The Mothers Movement Online*.

compared to her brother's, or her cousin's, or her father's, or even other girls' bodies. The moment may have gone something like this:

It's a hot summer's day and like every summer for as long as she can remember, Martha is spending a few weeks at her grandmother's house, playing in the fields and orchards with her cousins, splashing in the lake that they share with a neighbor.

Sweating under the sun and heat, in a rare moment of rest between rounds of play, she and her cousins John and Matt are laying under the gorgeous sky, their shirts shed like snake skins jumbled on the hot grass beside them. It is a scene that has repeated itself every summer without event... until this, her 6th year.

Suddenly a second-story window flies open with a bang at the rear of the house and all three children sit up and turn to see their grandmother leaning out to yell, "Martha Jean Gimble, *have you no shame?!* You put your shirt on this instant!"

Martha, mouth dropping open in silent shock, looks to Matt and John, waiting for them to receive a similar reprimand that never arrives. The boys stare back at her with the same confusion.

Her face hot, Martha crawls over to grab her pink tank top from the pile and wrestle it over her head, to cover shoulders, flat chest and belly—a profile none too different from her cousins' torsos. They look the same and yet weirdly, she must cover up while Matt and John can continue enjoying the cooling breeze on their exposed skin.

Another woman shared this story with me:

Ann was preparing for a high school talent show. A high achiever and straight-A student, she was used to doing well at whatever she put her mind to. For the talent show she would be performing a choreography her friend had created, that had been well-received when *she* performed it.

They worked and rehearsed together, until Ann could mimic her friend's movements flawlessly. She was ready for the stage.

She performed the dance in the talent show. People clapped, of course, but she didn't place. She won no award, which for her was out of character. Her mother thought she might know the reason. "Ann, you danced well, but you were too sexy. The judges didn't like it."

Ann was utterly confused. *Sexy?* That was the furthest thing from her mind. She had done the dance exactly as her friend had; it wasn't a sensual dance. There were no suggestive moves. No one had said those words about her lithe, blonde friend. The only thing she could attribute it to was the fact that Ann looked different: her hair was dark and thick, and although they were only a year or two into high school, she already had a curvy body, with big breasts and rounded hips.

Ann decided then and there that she would never be accused of being too sexy, again, since that, clearly was not a good thing. She never danced again, focused exclusively on math and sciences and became an engineer, and kept anything feminine or curvy about her under tight wraps.

Each of these stories represents a trauma in these girls' lives. They were not violent ones physically, but each took on a story from those events that then made them feel like there was something inherently wrong with them, wrong with the very bodies that they inhabited. A door within them shut.

When you do add violent trauma to the mix, the messages get buried deeper, cut with a sharper edge. The statistics are staggering around what percentage of women have experienced some sort of assault, especially sexual:

> One in five women and one in 71 men will be raped at some point in their lives.[7]

---

[7] Black, M. C., Basile, K. C., Breiding, M. J., Smith, S .G., Walters, M. L., Merrick, M. T., Stevens, M. R. (2011). The National Intimate Partner and Sexual Violence Survey (NISVS): 2010 summary report.

In the U.S., one in three women and one in six men experienced some form of contact sexual violence in their lifetime.[8]

91% of victims of rape and sexual assault are female, and nine percent are male.[9]

Suffice it to say that sadly—no, appallingly—sexual violence against women is the norm rather than the exception.

An experience I'll never forget is being in a room with 400+ women; packed into an auditorium for Mastery, the first course in the School of Womanly Arts. I don't remember what topic brought us to that moment—just that a woman was at the mic, crying, sharing her story of incest. We cried with her.

Mama Gena, who held the microphone for her, put a hand on the woman's shoulder and thanked her for her courage in sharing. Then she looked up and around at all of us sitting on the edges of our red velvet seats, crying. She asked to stand to stand in solidarity with our sister if we had ever experienced an assault, a trespass, a harassment, an unspeakable hurt of this nature.

Nearly every woman stood, including myself. I cried even harder, in shock. Because of course I know the numbers, I was a gender studies major in college, for fuck's sake.

But to SEE it. Visceral. On the faces and the bodies of nearly every woman in that auditorium. My soul wailed in rage and grief.

This is the lie we have been sold, the lie we've told ourselves: that our shame was unique. Private. Individual. "What was wrong with me that this happened? *How did I bring this upon myself?*" We still live in a

---

[8] Smith, S. G., Chen, J., Basile, K. C., Gilbert, L. K., Merrick, M. T., Patel, N., ... Jain, A. (2017). The National Intimate Partner and Sexual Violence Survey (NISVS): 2010-2012 state report.

[9] Rennison, C. M. (2002). Rape and sexual assault: Reporting to police and medical attention, 1992-2000 [NCJ 194530].

world that, when a woman is raped, she is asked what she was wearing, what she had had to drink, how loudly and violently she protested, how well she knew her attacker? (Usually, she did.) *Has any man ever had to answer these questions when mugged?*

One more statistic:

> Perpetrators of sexual violence are less likely to go to jail or prison than other criminals. Out of every 1,000 rapes: 310 are reported to the police; 57 lead to arrest; 11 get referred to prosecutors; 7 cases will lead to a felony conviction; and only 6 rapists will be incarcerated.[10]

The fact that it is a real, public, shared experience by the majority of women. That it goes largely unpunished. *That is no private shame, my friends. That is SYSTEMIC.* And yet another reason I say: *Women leaders?* MORE, PLEASE!

So how does living in a culture where violence against women is ordinary, acceptable, and somehow our fault, impact the way we show up in the world?

We are shamed and endangered for the very bodies in which we reside. And make no mistake: *you are your body*. As much as we try to operate from the neck up alone, as much as we try to deny her, there is no separating from your body without also vacating the physical plane.

To be shamed about something so inextricably connected to who we are, or around something about which we have no control—others' reactions to our bodies—is itself a crying shame. One door after another

---

[10] This statistic combines information from several federal government reports as compiled by RAINN (Rape, Abuse & Incest National Network): Department of Justice, Office of Justice Programs, Bureau of Justice Statistics, National Crime Victimization Survey, 2010-2014 (2015); Federal Bureau of Investigation, National Incident-Based Reporting System, 2012-2014 (2015); Department of Justice, Office of Justice Programs, Bureau of Justice Statistics, Felony Defendants in Large Urban Counties, 2009 (2013).

shuts within ourselves. For real reasons, that have to do with safety, and protection, and self-preservation, from actual, physical danger.

It takes energy to keep those doors shut.

And those shut doors start infiltrating every part of our lives where there is risk of exposure, of vulnerability. So that although we're thinking, what the fuck? I'm just trying to publish a blog post here, what is up with all this resistance I'm feeling?

Just know: you're not crazy.

And: the more of us that step forward, that tell our truth, that expose ourselves in spite of our fears and past experiences, *anyway*—the more this paves a different path for the generations of women to come. The girls who watch you, right now, to see how you show up.

Deeply embedded, internalized shame stories infiltrate every aspect of how we operate, in business and life. Stories that live in the very cells of our bodies. Stories that whisper (or shout): *No good. Ugly. Fat. Stupid. Not enough. Too much. Ridiculous. Scary. Exposure is scary. Vulnerability means violence.*

This book offers the antidote for all that. It is about showing up as ALL of who we are, *without shame,* to:

- Take a stand for our pleasure and self-care.
- Serve our purpose here on the planet.
- Reconnect with our bodies.
- Be visible in who we are and what we are here to do.
- Share our message.

Which is where shame intersects with your marketing... and with fulfilling your purpose on the planet. Every voice counts.

#Metoo is only the beginning.

Every woman who tells her unvarnished, unabashed truth brings us a step closer to a balanced world that honors Feminine wisdom, experience, history and contribution as equal to Masculine.

And yep... it is unfailingly intertwined with your brand, message, and copy.

MY STORY

> *I huddled in a small closet under my bunk bed. My tiny fingers had pulled the sliding door of the closet as far shut as I could from the inside, leaving a slim, bright crack through which I watched the open bedroom door.*
>
> *My pursuer appeared at the door and paused, eyes scanning, fist curled around a wire hanger, the sharp sting of which I knew well. Horrified that I would be found, I squeezed into the corner.*
>
> *Clamped eyes shut. Froze perfectly still. Held breath...*
>
> *The closet door remained shut. The bedroom doorframe, again empty. I had avoided danger.*[11]

I learned from a very young age that, quite literally, to be seen was dangerous. Hiding and silence kept me from harm.

The beatings were not a consequence of a behavior; I never knew what would precipitate them. So my little self thought, *It must be me.*

All I knew was that there was something darkly different about me, something that must be punished—confirmed when one of my mother's older friends looked me over with an appraising eye and said, "She's not beautiful, but you watch out for this one." I was eleven. And *hello*, within earshot! I may not have been "beautiful," but I wasn't deaf! I felt offended even though I didn't understand exactly what the woman meant, only that it wasn't good, and vaguely dangerous.

Once I was too big to hit, the rebukes came verbally—and after puberty, they changed in nature, from *stupid* and *useless*, to *whore*.

---

[11] Excerpt from my chapter, *Warrior Woman,* in *Courageous Hearts.*

Those lessons melded together and carried forward with me, like a backpack of useless supplies I hadn't yet realized I didn't need. I internalized them, though I may not have been able to articulate it; in my depths, I thought the abuse was my fault. For having that mysterious, dangerous quality. For a something wrong with me at my core. For being who I was.

So when the cook in the restaurant where I worked pressed me to him with arms thick with muscle and stuck his tongue in my mouth, I froze, and was silent.

So when, living on my own in Paris and riding the Métro to class, a white-haired businessman switched his briefcase from one hand to the other so he could properly grope me between the legs, and when the doors slid open, and to my horror, we were framed—*just so*—for the whole train station to see, his arm halving my body and ending in my crotch, I was again: Silent. Frozen. Humiliated.

And later, when a boyfriend shamed me for "letting" these things happen to me, his mouth curling in disgust, a part of me agreed, *He's right.*

My journey from hiding to visibility began when I started to unbind these stories from who I am—even seeing the gifts in the crappy stuff—one teeny-tiny baby step at a time. I have done a lot of work to get *here,* from hiding in a closet to nationally award-winning performer, from frozen silence to *this book*.

So believe you me when I tell you that *there is no judgment here*. I was the *queen* of hiding in plain sight, and can be kicked into a shame spiral as easily as anyone, anytime. The only difference between where I was and where I am now, is that I've had a lot more practice with tools that have built up my shame resilience.

If I can do this, you absolutely can, too.

MY STORY, REWRITTEN

That story, the hiding = safety story… I cannot express the hold it had over me, and how ashamed I felt that I couldn't seem to shake it.

Underneath that shame lay my real shame: that somehow I had brought that violence upon myself. That little girl that hid, baby Charisse, felt fundamentally flawed. How else could I understand the abuse? Except that there must have been something terribly wrong with me to cause someone who said they loved me to also hurt me.

(True story: it wasn't until decades later, when I worked with my first therapist in my early twenties, that I realized that there was a difference. "But I know she loves me," I would sob, as I grappled with the slow, deep realization that an early life steeped in terror is not every child's lot.

My therapist gently asked, "Did you ever consider that someone can love you, but not act in a loving way?"

Mind. Blown.)

That memory of me, hiding in the closet, *owned* me, for years. It seemed like anytime I did any personal development work around my own visibility, my own desire to take up more space in the world, I was led right back to that moment in the closet. I was playing an epic game of whack-a-mole with this one freaking memory that kept popping up: tiny me, crouching in fear, in a minute space that ballooned darkly around me except for that sliver of light, upon which my life depended. Breathless, terrified of being found. It wasn't memories of the repeated violence, or putting my body in front of my siblings' bodies, absorbing rains of blows myself, that imprisoned me in its grip—it was that single, paralyzed, silent moment. And the seeming lessons it carried: *Hold still. Don't breathe.*

If you let them see you, you're dead.

This terror has a long and colorful history. Many of us have the same fear, and it goes back generations. Lisa Lister calls this terror the witch's wound.[12] So many women throughout history were destroyed for being seen, for being who they were, for expressing their desire, their truth. Witches and midwives, wise women who practiced the old

---

[12] Lister, L. (2017). *Witch: Unleashed. Untamed. Unapologetic.* California: Hay House, p.85.

ways, burned at the stake; wives committed to asylums for disagreeing with their husbands or refusing to have sex; suffragettes beaten for demanding the vote for women; women stoned for dishonoring their families by falling in love, or girls' genitals sliced to prevent their ever feeling pleasure, even to this day. Joan of Arc, left to die at the hands of her captors, despite her contributions. The examples could fill their own books, and have.

Since patriarchy came into its own—only a few thousand years since a time when the Goddess was revered, and women along with her—thousands of women have been slaughtered, imprisoned, assaulted and abused for threatening the new "natural order."

So with this weighty history (and patterns that still continue today), is it surprising that when it comes time to show ourselves, we retract? Those women's screams are in our DNA, that trauma passed down through generations, indoctrinating us with cautionary tales. (*See what happens when you're different, when you contest the norms, when you speak up?*) And if you'll go there with me: How many of us *were* those women, in past lives?

How could that moment in the closet not have such a hold on my psyche, connected as it was to a primal, inherited history of hiding to keep safe? I despaired of ever releasing the hold this trauma held over me. Therapy, tapping, shamanic journeys, movement, Tantric massage—techniques that had worked elsewhere failed here.

Until.

Until I was challenged to rewrite my story. In an audience of hundreds at a 3-day personal development event, the speaker asked us to pretend we have amnesia, and rewrite a life story—especially one that held us in its limiting grip. A snide voice inside my head smacked her lips. *Hmph. You don't need this. You've done this work before.* I could see my internal know-it-all, settling back in her chair and crossing her arms firmly across her chest.

However, having been on the self-awareness path long enough to recognize when my ego is trying to trick me into staying cozy in my comfort zone (hey, her foremost job is to protect me; I get it), I tried a different approach.

You know what? I responded internally, picking up pen and poising it over the page. *What the heck. Let's just see what happens.* I put pen to workshop booklet, scribbling between images of the slides. I took my hands off the wheel, and just let my hand move; I had no idea what would emerge. Then, as if writing itself, this poured out of my pen:

> *I ran up the stairs and down the hall, turning into my bedroom as I heard my pursuer's footfalls creak at the bottom of the stairs. I had a good head start on her! I stuffed myself into the closet under my bunk bed, stifling giggles so she wouldn't find me. In the dark, I pressed my eye against the tiny crack I'd left between sliding door and frame, holding my breath, bursting with the secret of where I was.*
>
> *The petite woman appeared at in the doorway. "Come out, come out, wherever you are," she called in a sing-song voice, a smile playing on her lips as she pretended she had no idea where I could be.*
>
> *I couldn't wait through the charade of her checking every* other *hiding place before this one. I threw back the door and jumped out, announcing, "Here I am!" Arms and legs flung wide, my body marked the spot "X."*
>
> *Bending to me, arms outstretched, her hands grasped me firmly under the arms and swung my body up in an arc as my legs flew, free. Then, twirling, she tucked me in close at her waist. We cuddled close and laughed, sharing the private joke:* that's *not how you play hide-and-seek!*

The last paragraph is hardly decipherable in my notes. By that point, tears streamed down my cheeks as my hand wrote of its own accord.

I felt the shift, visceral and immediate: an internal reorganization, as my mind embraced this alternate reality that was somehow, magically, just as plausible as the remembered one. The jagged edges of an old wound cauterized, generated new flesh, and for the first in a long time, lay quiet, stunned into healing.

Memory is malleable like that. It's not to say that the original memory, the "truth" is invalid; it's that—well, in that moment I realized that in some alternate universe, a blink of an electron away, my rewritten story was just as potentially valid, and just as potentially true. (Thank you, quantum physics). I was free.[13]

ꟷ ꟷ

ACTION STEP: *What shame story is in your driver's seat?*

Shame and the marks of trauma thrive in secrecy and darkness. Expose them to the light, reveal a piece of your woundedness and it shrivels, losing its power.

"Life stories do not simply *reflect* personality. They *are* personality, or more accurately, they are important *parts of* personality, along with other parts, like dispositional traits, goals, and values," writes Dan McAdams, a professor of psychology at Northwestern University, along with Erika Manczak, in a chapter for the *APA Handbook of Personality and Social Psychology.*[14] How we interpret and recount the events of our lives matters.

What's coming up for you? What was a pivotal moment in your life, large or small, when a switch flipped? When you felt betrayed by your

---

[13] The power of story and rewriting the narrative is supported by science. Check out *Remapping Your Mind: The Neuroscience of Self-Transformation through Story* by Lewis Mehl-Madrona, MD, PhD with Barbara Mainguy, MA (Vermont: Bear & Company, 2015).

[14] Beck, J. (August 2015). Life's Stories: How you arrange the plot points of your life into a narrative can shape who you are—and is a fundamental part of being human. *The Atlantic.*

body? When a door shut to a part of yourself? When you started to hold a piece of yourself back?

There is power behind that shut door, bound energy in that hidden piece of yourself. Releasing the hold these stories have over us allows us to reclaim that power and energy.

Journal your story out. And if the tears come, the rage comes, all the better. Let it all out. Your emotional expression is your *power,* not your weakness.

If this is one of your first times acknowledging this story, take some time with it. Give yourself some space before taking the next step: rewriting it.

If however, your story is like mine was, bearded and mossy and wrinkled in its recurrence—oh, this old thing?—you may be ready to try rewriting it.

In either case, take note of the method I used in rewriting my story, known as automatic writing. Clear your mind. Take a few cleansing breaths. Meditate or pray for a few minutes, whatever your practice, and release any attachment or control over what's to flow as your pen moves across the page. (Important: this is actual pen, pencil, or even crayon on paper, not fingertips at keyboard. This activates different pathways in the brain.) It may take a little practice before you truly feel like you've relinquished control, but you will be amazed what emerges when you relax and let your intuition, your inner knowing, your guides, take the wheel.

SISTERHOOD AMPLIFICATION: ***Share your story with a friend.***

Ring up a good friend, the person you know who loves you unconditionally, and share the story with her.

More often than not, when you share your story, what you'll hear is, "Me too." We have so many common experiences that should be ancient history by now.

Or: Share your story with me. I can't tell you how often women, upon meeting me for the first time, share their innermost stories with me—stories they've often never shared before. I extend to you the same invitation. Email me at shamelessauthor@gmail.com, with the subject line "My story." Your words are safe with me.

EXTRA CREDIT: *Write a letter to your younger self.*

Starting in my teens, a weird pain in my left lung would catch me, holding me fixed and paralyzed like a frog pressed under glass. (I know, *that's* not psychosomatic at *all*). It felt as if something sticky had caught in my lung tissue, impossibly gluing the sides of my lung together like chewing gum. In order to again breathe freely, I'd either have to hold my breath and wait for the catch to dissolve on its own (which rarely worked), or I'd have to rip through the sensation, painfully.

In my 20's, I started seeing a therapist, and connecting dots between past and present. *And then I got that pain again*. My intuition flashed on an image of me as a little girl. I pulled my journal out and began to write. "Dear Charisse," I started.

I felt kind of silly, like I was playacting a scene out of a movie, but I continued, writing a letter to the little girl that hid in the closet. I could see her sitting in a little play chair, hands on closed knees, so prim, *so contained*. So quiet—that part of her, anyway. Other parts kicked and screamed and rebelled, but that part, with the big dark eyes under too-long bangs was quiet and fearful.

You were a good girl. You are *a good girl,* I whispered and wrote at the same time, and the tears began to spill. *It wasn't your fault,* I scrawled. *It's ok, it was never your fault.*

There was nothing wrong with you. There is *nothing wrong with you.*

In my imagination, I crawled into the dark closet with her, and pulled her little body into my lap, cradling her.

I love you, I finished. *You are safe now.*

My brain could not wrap around what difference this act would make, but something in me shifted. I felt lighter, somehow.

That sticky, lung-tearing pain never returned.

If this exercise speaks to you, write a letter to your younger self, knowing what you know now; express what you wish you knew then.

ഇ ഗ

What would happen if one woman told the truth
about her life?
The world would split open.

— Muriel Rukeyser

4

The shame-body connection

Reconnecting with your loyal consort

Knowing that we've been taught to feel shame about our very bodies, about qualities that define who we are as women, is it any wonder that most women leaders operate from the neck up?

Meaning: In our heads, thinking and talking our way through every act and decision, disconnected from the smelly, sweaty, crevice-y body attached from the neck down. We have been taught that a heady, rational approach is the "right" way to do things, especially in business and professionally.

Conversely, we have been taught to feel much shame around our bodies, those much-maligned and ignored, lambasted and oft-abused vessels—especially our curves, edges, and juicy bits.

Jungian psychoanalyst Clarissa Pinkola Estés calls our bodies our "loyal consorts."

A consort who remains loyal despite how we treat her. And how we treat her! We make her wait when she needs to pee, stuff her, starve her, dehydrate her, deprive her of sleep, caffeinate and pump her full of sugar when she's exhausted, and all manner of horrors we would never inflict on a loved one. Yet we subject our bodies to this treatment, on the regular. At certain points in my life, if I wasn't paying attention, I would catch myself doing all of the above to my sweet body in a single day!

Whenever I need a Wise Woman injection, I binge-listen to Dr. Estés. I sit at her knee and wrap my shoulders in her warm voice and soul-truth stories—via Audible, anyway.

In *The Joyous Body*, Clarissa writes that the body stores memories.[15] It tucks away history and experience, as I've witnessed time and again over years working with women's bodies:

A sudden adolescent growth spurt or blossoming of breasts marks itself in the hunched curve of a shoulder, a protection learned against the resulting unwanted attention and teasing.

An unforgotten betrayal holds the lips in a closed, flat line, determined to never again let anyone in, or near enough to repeat the experience.

The stifled emergence of sexuality, squelched by a moment's careless word or disapproving look by a parent, teacher, partner, or anyone we considered an authority, freezes the hips into a fixed, unmoving undercarriage—disallowing their natural sway and roll with a hold that requires a tremendous amount of energy to maintain.

In fact, all of these examples of past hurts, imprinted on the body, *suck energy*. Energy that could otherwise flow into creativity, expression, movement.

The body's untold stories shape how we carry ourselves and decide whether we open ourselves to new experiences—or, unwittingly, block the opportunities we so fervently desire. In other words, the body, with

---

[15] Estés, Clarissa Pinkola. *The Joyous Body: Myths & Stories of the Wise Woman Archetype, Dangerous Old Woman* Series, #3. Sounds True (2011).

For more on how the body stores memory, see Dr. Christiane Northrup, *Women's Bodies, Women's Wisdom: Creating Physical and Emotional Health and Healing,* and Dr. Bessel Van Der Kolk, *The Body Keeps the Score: Brain, Mind, and Body in the Healing of Trauma.*

its unspoken beliefs tacitly absorbed over a lifetime (but especially in our childhood), *surpasses conscious thought every time*.

Let that sink in. What does that mean?

A body whose story contradicts what you consciously desire will block your desire's attainment. For example, let's say that you want to attract your ideal audience with your messaging. If the story embedded in your body is one of a child who believes itself unworthy of love, how effective can that messaging be? *How much love will you be willing to let in?*

Here's another way to put it—memories, stored in the body, are like your operating system, much of which has been installed by age 7, during which time we accept as truth everything we see around us. According to Dr. Bruce Lipton's research[16], it's a matter of survival; there is so much to learn in order to integrate with our families and societies, our brains are in the same theta state they are in during hypnosis—in other words, we are in a state of unfettered absorption and unquestioning acceptance.

If we think about these early-life lessons as being our factory-installed operating system, the problem only arises when we're trying to install a new, incompatible app—say, a different belief about how lovable we are, or how much wealth we deserve to receive, that contradicts that early training (or operating system).

So, for example, let's say you make the business decision to launch a new program this year, aiming to bring in more revenue than you ever have before in your business. If this new level of abundance is in discordance with the messages you received early in life, it's like trying to install an app where the operating system isn't compatible. You can download the program, and valiantly try to run it; but it may stall, go buggy, or fail altogether. Our typical reaction is to look at the new

[16] You can get an introduction to Dr. Lipton's epigenetics work at ShamelessMovement.com/bookresources.

stuttering software as the problem, rather than an operating system that needs to be updated.

If we take the hardware analogy a step further: although a good deal of our "programming" occurs in early life, there are updates to the operating system that can impact whether or not we succeed with new goals and ideas. Every experience leaves its mark on us, positive or negative, *our choice.* A recent perceived business failure—or personal upset, like a divorce or other loss—can mark itself on our bodies, and quietly, behind the scenes, direct us toward self-sabotage and playing small, until we fully integrate the experience. (I give you tools for doing so in later chapters.)

All too often, we believe that our scars, our internalized stories, are invisible, undetectable by the outside world. But we are like satellite dishes, transmitting and receiving information at a depth and scope we rarely acknowledge, especially at the unconscious, bodily level.

So, people *see us*, see what we're saying, whether we like it or not. Their bodies' stories respond to our bodies' stories. Even if it's once-removed, as in the story we write with our marketing, and how that marketing is received. Or the way a team member responds to your directive—your words may say one thing while your body language says another.

So, how do we change the factory-installed operating system (or later unconscious updates) to match our newer goals and ideals, if there are contradictions between them?

The key is in taking ownership of the stories our bodies are telling. The question becomes: What stories do you *want* your body to tell? What stories is she telling right now? Is there discord between the two—and how do your early- (or not-so-early) life stories shape the story that you tell in your leadership, mission, and marketing?

I learned about my own body's unspoken stories firsthand when I trained for a national bellydance competition. And learned, too, that there is no distinction, between body and story, cell and memory. "Mind-body-spirit" is redundant. Each is the other; there is no separation.

My coach David and I had been working together for months in preparation. He pointed out ways I was holding back in my dance. As a longtime instructor, I maintained precise control. I had even trained myself, unconsciously, to dance just a hair ahead of the music—so that when my students followed, they would be right on time. David and I were trying to loosen the grip my teacher-body had on my artist-body.

One session changed my dance forever. David and I had been focusing on strengthening my shimmy, the quintessential bellydance move, a joyous vibration through the hips. He had given me techniques to practice, and my shimmy had improved but was still... *restrained.*

Reviewing that week's homework, a video recording of the latest version of my choreography, David hesitated, then asked quietly, "Can I ask you a personal question?"

We were Skyping, he in San Diego, me in suburban Chicagoland. Surprised, I nodded wordlessly.

"Was your last relationship... controlling?" he asked, tentatively.

Suddenly the tears flooded, and I stepped away. My shoulders quietly shuddered off-screen while David agonized that he may have lost one of his prized students.

It was true. A longtime lover, now ex, had followed me constantly when we first dated, insecure and jealous. Over the years that we were together, I became a smaller and smaller version of myself that I didn't recognize. In so doing I was trying to win his love, but this only seemed to infuriate him. Underneath and before that, my childhood had been terrorized by a close relative's violent fits of rage, perfectly preparing me to accept the same as "love" in later relationships.

The tears came when I connected that where I'd forgiven and released both my relative and ex years before, my body had internalized and still carried the message received from them: This body... uncontained... unrestrained, is "too much," "out of control," *shameful.*

Both had humiliated and punished me for a sensuality they found dangerous. I could convince neither that I was loyal and honorable.

I had learned a tightrope walk born of fear and shame, so customary it felt like home.

I wiped my eyes and returned to the screen. David let out a sigh of relief.

A tension I didn't even know existed, unclenched. *A dam broke*. My hips rocked and pistoned with a vigor and freedom I had never achieved in 10 years of practice. Hot damn! Now, I could put an eye out with that shimmy! And it only took a moment's watershed realization to free it.

I unleashed energy I hadn't realized was bound.

I went on to bring home a trophy in that national competition, unheard-of for a first-time participant.

What I have found, over years of studies and research in gender studies in college and beyond, and on-the ground experience dancing with women and hearing their stories, is this: though my story, like every woman's, is unique, it represents a common pattern.

A sidelong look, a hurled insult, a cutting parental observation, a drunken paw, a nonconsensual grope, an assault, a harassment—single or plural. Small, daily, incremental humiliations. Bullying. Rape. Incest. A blocked-out questionable memory. A suspicion. Even a past life or injury passed down through generations. In short, a trauma or sustained, chronic trauma over a period of time. Covered-up shames. Folded into the body, calloused and scarred into place. Or like a bullet or other foreign body, never removed and encased in layers of scars.

Often, these traumas are all tangled up with our feminine, sensual, sexual selves—so that both memory and sensuality get buried. Hushed. Replaced with robot parts that don't ooze and bleed and definitely don't shimmy.

Don't misunderstand—it's not just events or experiences perceived as negative that store in the body; positive ones do, too. Loving touch, kind words, fond memories, joyful movement, the births of children, all mark themselves upon the body. However, these happy "scars" do not typically limit or constrain our behavior the way that trauma and shame silently do.

Rather, we can harness that bodily power for healing and freeing energy, the same way I unleashed my shimmy. (I'll show you how.)

But first:

Where might *your* body be holding back floodgates or subtle shift, storing a memory that may predate language itself?

What untapped, sensual energy rests buried, bound, locked away under layers of shame?

Why bother walking this path at all? Because: What lies on the other side of shame?

Freedom. On the other side of shame is freedom.

And you, taking up more space and being more visible than you ever thought possible, attracting like a lightning rod the people, resources, and opportunities you desire.

Yassssss!

In the following chapters, we'll explore three critical areas of your brand story. First up, your unique value proposition, or how to "brag your brilliance," *shamelessly*. Second, we'll define your ideal client—which is as much about clarifying *your* desire as it about identifying who you uniquely serve. And finally, we'll get vulnerable (eek, it's that scary word!) and share your compelling story, the "why" behind your "what."

Your body is an untapped resource of intelligence, guidance and healing. *My approach merely taps what you already know at a cellular level.*

I call it Shameless marketing.

Or: *Joining the Shameless Movement.*

Your message begins in the body.

Your body, that sacred vessel, your living temple, is: A creative tool and resource. Communicator of your deepest intuitive wisdom. Holder of generations of wisdom, passed through your DNA. Your most steadfast supporter and unfailing advisor.

By getting out of your head (what I call your "little brain") and into your body (what I call your "big brain"), you will get clarity in a way you may have never experienced around your brand, message, and voice as a leader, not to mention around decision-making and impact.

This is about freedom, baby.

Let's get started.

ꝏ ꝏ

ACTION STEP: *Where do you hold back?*

Where *might* your body be holding back floodgates or subtle shift, storing a memory that may predate language itself?

Do you sense a buried, sensual energy, locked away?

Check in with your body: are there parts that are stiff? When you walk, do you let your hips sway? Do you suck your belly in?

Where are you self-conscious? Critical?

In your journal, write a letter to the body part that seems the most quiet, or shut down, or insistent. Then, write a letter, from her back to you. What messages does she have for you?

As my dear friend and wise woman Victoria Whitfield says, "Your imagination *is* your intuition"—so if you feel like you're making up her reply, *perfect.*

SISTERHOOD AMPLIFICATION: *Love her forward.*

As you get on speaking terms with your body, you'll start to realize how much you've neglected her. You'll also begin to notice when the ladies around you are less than kind to their bodies. Pay forward a little body love:

Compliment a woman on her "enviable curves" (to this day, one of my all-time favorite compliments received).

Tell her that her smile stops traffic; I have a friend whose smile is absolutely blinding it's so bright.

Compliment the perfect sway of her back, the fine muscle in her legs, the fineness of her wrists.

Sounds weird, doesn't it? We're so used to receiving these compliments only in the context of pick-up lines and come-ons.

Avoid comparison—the other way we're used to giving and receiving compliments. "I wish I had your waist." "You're so skinny, I wish I could fit into those jeans!" Or as my favorite Chicago dancer used to say to me, teasingly. "*That hair...* You bitch, I hate you*!*"

What if we made it a sacred practice to notice and acknowledge the beauty of the women around us?

And hey: it's not the reason that you do it, but what goes around comes around. The more appreciation you spread, the more your own cells will soak in the love.

ꙮ ꙮ

Don't say things. What you are *stands over you the while, and thunders so that I cannot hear what you say to the contrary.*

—Ralph Waldo Emerson

5

Your message begins in the body

The power of body language

Before we can have more impact with our messaging and take up more space in our branding, a fair question to ask is how are we taking up space in the body? What story is your body broadcasting right now?

We often talk about how we communicate with others through our body language—but what about the nonverbal cues we send ourselves?

As I talk about in my book, *Every Day Pleasure,* a smile doesn't simply communicate pleasure to the outside observer:

> *Pleasure begins in the body. Smiling, in particular, sends signals to our brain that say, "I'm happy."*
>
> *It works like this: when we feel happy, we smile. And when the muscles that form our smile contract, it gives feedback to our brain that says we're happy. In essence, smiling creates a "pleasure loop"—the opposite of a vicious circle.*

By harnessing the power of the body and smiling, we tip our mood toward happy.[17]

So, too, can we set the stage for boldly stating our value and attracting the results we want, by holding the body in a way that expresses confidence, ease, passion and enthusiasm; qualities that forecast success in a study shared by Amy Cuddy in her book, *Presence:*

> *Visiting student Lakshmi Balachandra had been investigating the way entrepreneurs make pitches to potential investors and the way investors respond. After meticulously analyzing videos of 185 venture capital presentations—looking at both verbal and nonverbal behavior—Lakshmi ended up with results that surprised her: the strongest predictor of who got the money was not the person's credentials or the content of the pitch. The strongest predictors of who got the money were these traits:* confidence, comfort level, and passionate enthusiasm.[18]

When people feel passionate and confident, their body language is expansive. *They take up more space*—with posture, gestures and stride. When people feel powerless, they fold in on themselves: "limbs touching torso, chest caved inward, shoulders slumped, head lowered, posture slouched," Cuddy explains.

The same body language cues that tell observers how to feel about us, also communicate with our own brains, providing feedback about how we feel about *ourselves*. When you fold in on yourself, you feel powerless and less influential.

---

[17] Sisou, Charisse. *Every Day Pleasure: A bellydancer's perspective on how to add more time, fun and passion, daily.* Download your copy at ShamelessMovement.com/bookresources.

[18] Cuddy, Amy. *Presence: Bringing your boldest self to your biggest challenges.* Little, Brown & Company (2015).

Try it. First, do a quick check-in: How are you sitting now? Are you slouched or hunched over, are your legs crossed, are your arms crossed? Are you taking up more space, perhaps with legs open or back straight?

Next: Sit erect, throwing your arms up overhead in a big "V" for victory, as if you've won a race. Hold this position for a solid minute or two. Notice how your shoulders are naturally thrown back, how your torso and ribcage expands, how you become instantly taller. *Most importantly, notice how you feel.*

This first, victorious position, known as "Pride," is engrained in us—as Cuddy explains in her TED talk[19], where she substantiates that yes, our body language provides feedback that can grow our own sense of power and confidence. Even people who were born without sight will make this same gesture upon completing a physical challenge, never having seen it before.

Next, try the opposite. Sag your shoulders forward and curl in. Cross your legs at the knees or ankles. Pull your elbows into your torso, and cup an elbow in the palm of your opposite arm. Cover your neck protectively with your free hand. *Now, how do you feel?*

As Cuddy points out and as you may have felt even as you changed poses, the habitual postures we take differ along gender lines. The latter crossed pose *feels more feminine.* Historically and chronically powerless, women are more likely to make their bodies smaller to *take up less space*.

BODY LANGUAGE AND GENDER

Cuddy describes the difference, and when girls start to carry themselves differently:

---

[19] Cuddy, Amy. *Your body language may shape who you are*.

> Anyone who's observed young children might have noticed that both boys and girls use expansive postures and movements. Unconstrained by cultural norms, little girls seem to be just as likely as little boys to throw their arms in the air, stand with their shoulders back, and plant their feet apart. But at some point this appears to change: boys continue to expand, and girls begin to collapse.
>
> When my son entered middle school, I watched his female friends change the way they carried themselves. They began to draw their bodies inward, hunching their shoulders, wrapping their arms around their torsos, twisting up their legs and ankles, and lowering their chins.

Young children are naturally open; they have perfect posture without needing to be told. It is only through picking up the body language of the people around them do they learn to slouch.

Over ten years of moving with women as a bellydance instructor, I witnessed the stories we carry in our bodies. The rounded shoulders, the bowed heads, the bellies held in so as not to reveal their roundness and softness. A stiffness around the hips, so as not to reveal sensual selves. Small concessions of power, subtle foldings in on ourselves.

To try to create an expansive, magnetic message in your copy while constricting the body doesn't make any sense; your body is the vehicle of your message, as well as its broadcaster. To write copy while folded in on oneself, to hone in on what makes you and your approach brilliant and unique on the planet while simultaneously trying to take up less space physically makes about as much sense as trying to travel the high seas in a sailboat with the sails furled up and the anchor firmly planted on the ocean floor. *It might look like you're sailing, but you're not going anywhere*.

POWER = CONNECTION

Cuddy clarifies that powerful body language does not mean dominating body language. In fact, the latter is repellent, while the former inspires connection.

Think about how much more willing you are to trust someone who makes eye contact, has an open and relaxed manner, and faces you. Cuddy's research confirms what our bodies intuitively know.

She writes, "It's about intimacy, not intimidation."

I absolutely love this idea for our purposes—because building trust and intimacy is exactly what we want to do with our words, whether for our businesses and organizations, with our teams, or with the people closest to us.

ꟾ ꟾ

ACTION PLAN: ***Check in with the body***

Remember the "Visibility Quotient" assessment from chapter 2? *Shame writes itself on the body.* Assessing your body's habits will give you more insight into whether shame is in the driver's seat more than you know.

(Download the PDF at ShamelessMovement.com/bookresources).

Rating on a scale from 1 to 5: *Checking in with my body, I tend to….*

① ⑤

___ Fold my arms....................................Gesture openly with my arms

___ Stand with feet together...............................Stand with feet apart

___ Round my shoulders..................................Roll my shoulders back

___ Suck my belly in...Let my belly go soft

___ Slouch..Throw my shoulders open

___ Clench my jaw...Relax jaw open

___ Grit my teeth...Let my teeth part

___ Hold my mouth pressed closed..............................Let my lips part

___ Take up less space...Take up more space

___ Default to "resting bitch face"..........Let a smile play over my lips

___ Walk with hips held stiff...................Let my hips sway when I walk

How did you do, out of a possible 55 points? For many of us, looking at the way we have internalized shame, documenting itself in the body, and subtly directing our body language, may be a new concept. For others, we may have done a lot of "work" on internalized concepts and limiting beliefs, but not necessarily had the physical awareness and practice of translating that work into the hidden messages transmitted by our bodies. This assessment measures both.

11 – 25: Dipping a Toe in Shameless Waters

Does this mean I'm shame-"full"? Never, my love. None of us are born with shame, or are "full" of it. Every single one of us was born shamelessly naked, and every single one of us has been marked by life differently.

Look back over the list of body check-ins, and pick the one that seems the easiest one to turn "shameless" – for example, simply make it a point to notice when you fold your arms and release them... Then, notice the feelings that come up. Do you feel exposed? A little nervous? More relaxed and open? Less defensive? Whatever the feelings, let them come and fully feel them.

26 – 40: Selectively Shameless

You have some great habits... and others that you may not have been aware of previously. Sometimes I find with my clients that their results fall in this category due to a more specific, localized shame—like the grief contained in a downturned mouth, or rounded shoulders as a vestige of early-life bullying.

I'm going to say something you may not expect: it's not even that important to know the "what" behind the embodiment of the shame. By practicing bodily habits in carriage and movement that align with the opposite of shame—openness, expansiveness, pride, self-worth, *freedom*, you release shame. (So magical!)

Which habit, revealed by the assessment, surprised you the most? Start there. Notice when it happens, then notice how you feel when you try the opposite. Like letting your lips part, with the barest hint of a smile, rather than holding your lips pressed together. See what shifts in your energy and the results of your interactions.

41 – 55: Boldly Shameless

Girrrrrrl! You are a shameless body language ninja! And, as we are infinite beings, there is always room to "press your edge" for refinement and improvement. Where did you score "low" that surprised you? In what area(s) of your body, as you scan over them, do you continue to sense resistance or disconnect? In what pockets do you continue to hold back? (We all have them, and they change day to day as we accrue new experiences.) What would it look like to stop holding back in those areas? Where can you go even deeper? Which prickly points rear their heads at unexpected moments? *So* exciting to explore.

For those of us who have experienced shame hopping in the driver's seat (and that would be, truly, all of us), we are each a member of what Clarissa Pinkola Estés calls "Scar Clan."

"Scar Clan membership comes from having lived through a great something," she writes. "... A gigantic group of souls who are in the midst of healing self and others, who at least halfway have reset their own bones, who still move with standing-room-only heart, despite certain fragilities that come from scar tissue aching at unpredictable times, many years after wounding."[20]

There is no shame in having these wounds and scar tissue. *We all have them*. And, by practicing a certain *shamelessness* with our bones and sinews, we can release the hold those wound and scars have on us.

---

[20] For a full description and definition of Scar Clan, see Estés' article, *Scar Clan: A Lost Story, Vatican II*, on the Book Resources page at ShamelessMovement.com.

SISTERHOOD AMPLIFICATION: *Compare notes with a friend.*

Doing the assessment, what did you notice? What did you experience? What did you feel? Share the assessment with a friend and compare findings.

ഇ ര

Stand up straight and realize who you are, that you tower over your circumstances.

—Maya Angelou

6

Your body as a creative tool

The well-resourced woman

By releasing shame stories, you free bound energy. To create. To shine. To be visible.

What is so powerful about the body is that—*you don't even need to know what the stories are.* It doesn't need to take years of therapy or soul-searching. *Transformation can be instantaneous*. Change the language of the body, tune in to its whispers (and shouts) and witness the body as it heals itself.

In a monthly women's circle I used to attend, one meeting we each took turns lying in the middle, head in one woman's lap while the rest circled around, laying hands on the body. It was a simple demonstration of how healing touch is... and how every woman is a healer. And it reminded me of slumber party games we used to play as kids.

It was my turn. I eagerly laid my head in Meredith's lap as, all around, ladies put a hand on shin here, upper arm there, on shoulder, belly, thigh. Their hands were warm and kind. I felt drowsy and safe. Meredith instinctively reached her hand out over my chest, but asked first, "Is it okay if I put my hand *here*?" Her palm hovered over the center of my rib cage, in between my breasts. I nodded my assent and she gingerly placed her hand just above cleavage.

Like a swarm of gathering bees, I felt the area under her hand buzz and spark, the energy gathering, then overflowing. Suddenly, I was crying—and not graceful, silent tears. A plaintive moan rose from my belly, and I heard my wailing, open-mouthed cries as if they came from someone else. My back arched under Meredith's hand as I sobbed. A few of the ladies, hearing my cries, sighed and teared.

Afterward, as we went around the circle, sharing what we experienced, the ladies looked at me expectantly. What memory had I unearthed? What was it? *Why did I cry?*

The truth was, *I had no idea.* At the soft edges of my awareness I suspected that it had to do with my mothering. My head cradled in a woman's lap, circled by mothers, a deep yearning cracked open. My mother rarely expressed her love physically when I was a child, though we hug now. She was not especially warm—or rather, she usually seemed too preoccupied or weary to bond, an overwhelmed divorcée.

I remember trying to put my head on her shoulder. We were in a van bumping along a road to her home town in the Philippines, at the tail end of a long journey from Chicago. I had had to pee since we boarded the first plane, more than 24 hours before, but having never been on a plane before I didn't know what to do and was afraid to ask, and afraid to get out of my seat. I retreated into silent stillness.

By the time we were in this closed van with a bunch of strangers, I was in so much pain, I wanted nothing more than to sleep until we arrived at our destination. (Even though I was the ripe age of 11, it never occurred to me to ask for what I needed; I'd long before learned to hide discomfort and desire.) I tilted my head to lean it on her shoulder, but we never cuddled, so I didn't know how to curl my body into hers. She made no move to put her arm around me or acknowledge the contact so we sat stoically next to each other, my head tilted at a 90-degree angle and bouncing on her hard shoulder at each rut in the road. Eventually I gave up and raised my head back up, my neck sore from trying.

The only time I did remember being held tenderly, just so, is when lice was going around school, and my sister and I were both affected. I lay my head in her lap as my mother combed through my thick hair for nits. It had been a rare moment of intimacy.

Though I could not articulate what had transpired in that circle of women, like Proust's madeleine, Meredith's hand had sparked layers of memory. There had been, undoubtedly, a healing. I felt open, warm, released, *more whole*.

Our bodies' natural tendency is toward heath and healing, physically and emotionally. Bring awareness and opportunity, and she can change in the blink of an eye.

Here are three, easy checkpoints to tune into, places in the body where tension and unconscious posture collect.

You can check in on these parts of your body right at your desk, before you put fingers to keyboard to write an email or LinkedIn profile, or get on the phone for a sales call.

YOUR MOUTH

Is it closed? Clenched? Tight?

Let your jaw relax, your lips part. Allow the corners of your mouth to tease up into the hint of a smile. This act, through its feedback loop, usually launches me into a full-fledged smile.

Another "hack" I use to relax your face? *Wink at yourself in a mirror.* It is impossible to keep a straight face!

Why is relaxing the mouth and jaw important? We press our lips closed in a flat thin line, or clench our jaws, when we are trying to protect and defend, keeping perceived danger *out.* Consequently, we also keep the good stuff from coming in, too. Pressed lips can also mean that we're holding something back—a truth or feeling.

Briefly, I offered body-scans at a yoga studio—like an intuitive oracle card reading, but of the body. The owner, challenging me, said, "Okay, let's see what you can do." I asked her to stand, then walk, and I watched from front, side and back. My eyes were immediately drawn to her mouth, which she held in a thin line—but it felt like there was something heavy there, so I went for the easier, lighter readings first. She had a very precise, almost prim gait, not uncommon for teachers in the physical arts—used to being scrutinized by their students, they get in the habit of being super-articulate and "perfect" in their movements, as an example for their students.

We practiced relaxing through the hips and shoulders, and I encouraged her to let her body walk with a less measured gait. Our time was nearly up, but my eyes kept returning to her mouth and jaw. There was a slight, almost imperceptible downturn at the corners of her mouth. Nervously, I blurted, "Your mouth..." Then asked, more gently, "What are you sad about?"

Tears welled in her eyes. "Unrequited love," she said, her eyes widening in shock at the admission. She had only just met me. She deeply loved a man whom she'd dated briefly, she explained, but he could not take their relationship further because his spiritual practice forbade it. I hugged her as she cried. She hastily wiped back tears.

Her body revealed truth. We think we're hiding, when we're not. We think we're sneaking into a room without anyone noticing us—and everyone sees us.

(You don't have to hide anymore.)

The only question is whether we choose to own the stories our bodies are telling, or not.

Let your people in. Soften the muscles around your mouth and jaw. Allow your mouth to soften. Let your lips part. As one of my teachers, the statuesque Israeli dancer Orit Maftsir said, "It's ok to let the audience know you're breathing."

YOUR SHOULDERS

Are they curled in? Rolled forward? Tense? *Let them roll open and down your back.* The opposite of hunched over is *not* to stand or sit ram-rod straight with your chest puffed out.

Why is rolling back the shoulders important? Because when people are afraid or feel powerless, they roll their shoulders inward, protectively, as we talked about in the last chapter. There is a direct correlation between how we express with the body and the words we choose to express ourselves.

Many women habitually round their shoulders, wearing their stories there. Perhaps she sprouted up faster than her classmates and was teased for towering over everyone else. Maybe she developed earlier than the other girls, or had a voluptuous bosom that drew unwanted attention. Maybe she was teased for being flat. One of the ladies in my community, Amy, had average-sized breasts, but her mother had struggled against assumptions made about herself because of her own large breasts. She passed her obsession onto her daughter: *Never show cleavage! Cover yourself up! Stop sticking them out like that!* Amy kept her arms crossed over her chest whenever at rest, and rarely wore anything cut below a modest V.

Notice where your shoulders are, relative to your neck. To release tension, scrunch your shoulders all the way up to your ears—then let them drop. Notice the warm flush as tension releases.

Turn your head from side to side, neck long and eyes soft like a regal queen. You can even gently nod your head as you look out over each shoulder. Feel the gentle twist in your neck, and listen to the (perfectly normal) small crackles and pops as you swivel your head.

Let your head drop to one side, ear toward your shoulder. Allow your head to roll from shoulder to shoulder, dropping chin to chest, and reverse. (Do this seated, or, if standing, let your knees soften as your head drops and rolls).

Soften and open your shoulders, rolling them back as if they're melting down your back. Feel your ribcage open and expand.

Amel Tafsout, an Algerian priestess masquerading as a bellydancer and one of my dance mentors, shared the analogy that your chest "is your sunshine." (Not, I would add, your *headlights.*)

Let this sink in. *Your sunshine.* Shoulder blades drop down the back as your torso fills and radiates like a beacon.

YOUR BELLY

Do you hold it? Suck it in? Cover it protectively with your arms? Feel self-conscious about it?

Amel calls this part of the body your "full moon." (Incidentally, your rear is your "half-moon." Isn't that nice?)

Renaming your parts helps to dismantle the vitriol we've hurled at our too thick this or too thin that or too *too* whatever.

When I taught a workshop at a pole dance studio and shared the "full moon" belly name, one of the young ladies cried out, "I hope not!" and placed a hand over her flat, muscled tummy.

Our cultural obsession with fit, taut bodies has undercut our natural softness—and accepting our full, soft belly, that is more than a "6-pack." (Or 12-pack, for women; our abdominal musculature is different than a man's.)

Your soft underbelly.

The center of your being.

The womb where we carry our children.

The fertile ground of creation.

Magical organs, cushioned, cradled, housed *here.*

We often pull our bellies in, trying to appear smaller than we are, or in protection.

Letting the belly go soft is an expression of self-acceptance: *I have nothing to hide.*

Of trust: *I have nothing to protect.*

Lisa Nichols started repeating a series of affirmations when she was a single mom turning her financial life around that I have found powerfully freeing. She would look herself in the eye in the mirror and say:

> *I have nothing to protect.*
> *I have nothing to prove.*
> *I have nothing to hide.*
> *I have nothing to defend.*
> *Now, who do I choose to be?*

She explains, "Your energy is consumed with protecting, proving, hiding and defending. But if you let go of that, *now you're in creation.* Every day I told myself that."[21]

Nichols' words speak directly to the underlying stories that keep us hiding and playing small. But *what if…*

What if you don't have anything to hide? Or protect? Or prove?

Let your belly go soft and witness what happens when you let your guard down. How can we be compassionate with our clients when we are not compassionate with ourselves? How can we be kind with the recipients of our services when we are not kind to ourselves?

This simple practice has been, for me, a physical expression of forgiveness. Of myself—and the people who have done me harm.

I no longer need to defend.

Whenever we release tension in the body, we remove obstacles to bringing the right people in, the right opportunities in, more of what we want in.

Whenever we release a story that's no longer true for us, dissolving old hurts—we regain the power that was bound up in those stories.

Like Lisa says, *now we're in creation.*

So we can show up bigger, and do what we are here to do with more energy, and less effort.

BONUS CHECK-IN: YOUR HIPS

Aww yeah… *We're going there*.

Just as uncovering the story of my hips helped me place in the Bellydancer of the Year competition, checking in and allowing your hips

---

[21] Listen to the whole talk on YouTube: *A STORY THAT WILL CHANGE YOUR LIFE - One of The Best Speeches Ever by Lisa Nichols (emotional).* I cry every time I watch it.

to freely move will unlock your presence and joie-de-vivre—and make you, and your message, that much more magnetic.

Try these movement experiments:

Shift your walk. Go ahead. Put the book down for a minute and walk across the room, just as you normally do. First, notice: do your hips sway as you walk? Or do you hold them tight and fast under you? There's a reason why I include how you walk in the assessment at the end of last chapter.

So often we are taught that only "fast girls" or girls who are "asking for it" allow their hips to wantonly sway, roll and jiggle. When I was in grade school, the girl who (rather adorably actually) let her hips tick-tock with her walk was nicknamed "Switch." No one else coveted that nickname. *We're taught, repeatedly and especially as we develop through adolescence, that the natural mechanics of our bodies are something "shameful" that should be restrained. That to inhabit our natural and powerful sensuality is dangerous.*

This, my loves, is bullshit.

The movement of our hips is our natural shock absorber (have back pain much?). But even more than our natural alignment and movement—our hips are the seat of our pleasure. It feels *good* to be fully present in our juicy undercarriage and let our weight shift fully from foot to foot as we walk, naturally rolling and swaying our hips.

By holding our hips fixed and unmoving, we prevent ourselves from being fully present as we move through the world. The ramifications are far-reaching:

I cannot overstate how important your pleasure, positive state of being and body freedom impacts your message. Your business results. Your decision-making ability. It is a necessary, required first step. (Without it, your results will hit a ceiling and plateau there, frustratingly, as you do "everything right" as your progress stalls.)

Earlier this year I presented this tool at a national conference to a roomful of professional organizers. It was early in the event, so—committed learners, all—they swayed the rest of the conference, winking at each other in the hallways like a secret sisterhood. When I saw them the next day, they reported what a difference this small change had made, in the way people responded to them, and most excitingly, in how they *felt.*

Try it. Don't overthink it. There's no right or wrong way to do this. You may have a walk more akin to a Mae West glide or a Marilyn Monroe jiggle; a take-no-prisoners J-Lo stance or juicy Beyoncé stride. Your walk is totally and beautifully unique to you.

For a deeper dive, check out my YouTube tutorial, "Sway your walk: one step toward radical acceptance of your beautiful feminine body," here: ShamelessMovement.com/bookresources.

Circle your hips. There are so many ways to play with this movement. Glide your hips around in a circle, as if you're tracing the inside of a hula hoop. Don't try to isolate them from the rest of your body—notice how leading with the hips deliciously tips and moves the rest of your body.

For a smaller, more intimate movement, circle your pelvis. This is something you can do seated, standing, or even lying down—I love doing this at my desk as I'm working, if I notice my energy flagging or focus straying. Notice how the movement tips the hips around in a small, more inward-facing circle. How it gently stretches and contracts, in turn: belly, obliques, back, obliques. So luscious!

Use the full body check-in tool—mouth, shoulders, belly, hips—anytime you feel resistance. Do it before you write a piece of copy, or email a prospect, or start a sales conversation. Witness how checking in with your body, releasing the tension there and uncorking your physical presence shifts and softens you as you market and sell—then witness the results. And tell me about them! I want to hear the difference these practices make in your business. Just email me at shamelessauthor@gmail.com.

Want more inspiration? Listen to Jen's story, and how connecting with her body impacted her business, at ShamelessMovement.com/bookresources.

ꕥ ꕥ

ACTION STEP: ***Make it a practice.***

Set reminders on your phone to do the body check-in I described throughout this chapter: mouth, shoulders, belly, and hips. Take a few moments to journal what you notice and how you feel.

SISTERHOOD AMPLIFICATION: ***Share this practice with a sister.***

Make a deal with a girlfriend that she also check-in with her body, and exchange what you observe.

You can synchronize your watches (or smartphones), superspy style, and check-in at the same time, and text each other what you notice. You can gently remind each other, hold each other accountable.

Notice how you hold your body, and your sisters hold theirs, when you're in circle.

Come up with ways to gently remind each other and model open, expansive body language. A gentle hand on the shoulder can nudge, *roll the shoulders back*. You can promise that every time you hug, you relax your bellies in tandem. (How cute is that?!)

I wrote the story myself. It's about a girl who lost her reputation and never missed it.

— Mae West

7

Brag your brilliance

Defining your unique value proposition

So, bragging may not be the most comfortable thing for you... *Yet.* (The purpose of this chapter is to change all that.)

If I haven't made it utterly clear yet, let me reiterate: *the goblins are real*. If every time you've taken another step to put yourself "out there" and heard the voices whisper, "Who do you think you are? Aren't YOU getting too big for your britches?" Know that *there is nothing wrong with you*. (There has never been anything wrong with you).

It means that you're human and female and have not been impervious to a constant onslaught of messages from family, parents, culture, religion, society, and more. *It's not your fault*.

Amplifying your visibility, however—including learning how to comfortably brag about yourself and your organization—*is your responsibility*.

Why?

Because you are totally unique. No, really: there has never been anyone like you—never, across time and history. Amongst billions of people, there is no one else like you, on the entire planet.

No one is as exceptionally suited to do what you do best, as you are.

And that uniqueness is tied to your purpose.

Before we go any further, let's get rid of any discomfort you have about bragging *right now*. I intentionally use the word "brag," to disrupt our long-held restrictions around it.[22]

I want to *change* the way you define bragging.

I am not suggesting that you become an insufferable braggart or begin boasting about how great you are to everyone within hearing. (To which you would be entitled, because, by the way, you *are* all that and a bag of chips).

When I say *brag*, I mean *own your gifts*.

Fully, without apology.

Without holding back.

Shamelessly.

That's why there's no such thing as competition, not really. There may be six landscapers in a chamber of commerce—but each is best suited to serve a different niche, each has a different personality, each is passionate about a different clientele. *It is by amplifying this uniqueness that we're better able to call out our right-fit clients*.

You bring your own array of natural aptitudes, learned skills, accomplishments and experiences, including life experiences—or as my friend Kim puts it, "diploma from the School of Hard Knocks"—that is unique to your professional and personal journey.

I mention natural aptitudes because, more often than not, your unique zones of genius are so natural and easy for you, *you take it for granted that not everyone is wired like you*. So much so, that in supporting a client through identifying her brags, she may not even recognize them as uncommon skills that few others have.

(Yep, you are that brilliant.)

[22] For a brilliant and deep dissertation of the power of bragging, see Thomashauer, Regena, *Pussy: A Reclamation,* or her earlier book, *The School of Womanly Arts,* published under her alias, Mama Gena.

You have skills with which you were born, or that you honed over thousands of hours, for example:

- Navigating classroom, laboratory or courtroom environments;
- Overcoming obstacles and language barriers as a new immigrant;
- Training and conditioning to climb mountains or run a marathon;
- Digesting complex information and translating it into lay terms;
- Putting people at ease, so they're quick to trust and build relationships with you;
- Building authentic, high-integrity relationships that later spawn high-performing loyal teams or strategic partnerships.

Often, clients come to me with the question, "What do I do?"

They know that their clients love whatever "it" is, but they have trouble articulating their differentiating factors—their "unique value proposition," a fundamental part of their brand story. *What makes them different. What it is that they truly offer.*

I call your unique value proposition something sexier (and more active): *bragging your brilliance.*

HOW TO FRAME YOUR BRAGS

1) Lead with results.

This was a simple guideline I learned in the resume writing world, where I was the behind-the-scenes writer for award-winning career coaches.

Leading with your results has powerful implications when you start to apply it to your copy. *Your people are most interested in the final outcomes of what you deliver.* Most of us, because we're such experts at what we do, lead with our process, the "what" that we do to help our clients achieve those results.

Some prompting questions:

What have you accomplished for your clients?

What are they now able to do or have since working with you?

What impact has your nonprofit had in the world?

After attending one of your talks, what is the audience able to do?

What were you able to do for your company as an employee?

2) Tell the story behind your brag.

A simple storytelling framework that powerfully positions your can be summed up in the acronym "CAR": Challenge, Approach, Results. More important than your individual/business accomplishments is how you achieved them—the how and why speaks volumes to who you are and why you're different.

Results: Identify these first. What are the top accomplishments, of which you are the most proud? Who are your three favorite clients and what did you help them achieve? What are your three biggest success stories?

Then reverse-engineer the stories leading in to them:

Challenge: What was the situation *before* you came in and worked your magic? Did you encounter any resistance to the change you were implementing? How did your client feel before working with you? *Set the stage*; what was the scenario?

Approach: How *you* solve challenges, versus the way someone else would approach the same situation, speaks to your unique value. How did you approach the issue? Did you build strategic relationships, leverage a system or technology, or break down a strategy into implementable action steps? Everyone takes a unique approach to a particular challenge—what was yours?

3) Stay relevant.

When you're bragging in a particular context—say, in a blog article—tie the brags to what is most relevant to your intended audience. For example, let's say you just achieved a weight-loss goal. That's great, but is it relevant, say, if you're an accountant?

On the face of it, no—unless you learned lessons along the way that *are* relevant to your peeps. Relate meal planning to budgeting around money, or the power of tracking what you eat and do is not far afield of tracking your revenue and expenses.

4) Stay in the body.

If you feel yourself slipping into your headspace as you go through these steps, getting bogged down in details or circling without landing, *stop.* Put pen or keyboard down. Get up and move.

Dance, stretch, hydrate, do something physical that brings you pleasure. (More juicy techniques coming in the next chapter).

When in doubt, *get into the body*.

When stuck, *get into the body*.

When stalling or procrastinating, *get into the body*.

She is your wisest counsel.

Ground, consult with her, then come back to task. *You've got this.*

5) Be specific.

Details give your audience something to hang their hat on. And details in your brags prevent you from trying to gloss over celebrating yourself by throwing out blanket statements. (It would be like saying "I brag that I'm healthy and active," versus "I brag that I climbed Mount Kilimanjaro—and survived to tell the tale!" The first doesn't spark much interest or curiosity—but the second does.)

6) Notice the patterns.

What are the recurring themes? What do you notice that you do again and again? The results that your clients have again and again? The problems that you solve over and over? These are all guideposts to your unique brilliance.

7) List gratitudes.

Who can you acknowledge for their support in reaching your goals? Who helped you along the way? Who do you admire? Who inspires you?

Give credit where credit is due, and notice how you've taken those lessons and made them your own. Taken a system and customized it to a particular market, or become the bridge to take a process to a wider or different audience.

Who are your mentors? What circumstances allow you to thrive?

Gratitude creates an expansive space around this practice of bragging our brilliance—what you appreciate in others holds clues to your genius. How do you echo what you admire in someone else? How do you contrast? What is the unique spin that you bring to predecessors' work in your industry? (For example, there are a lot of marketing books out there... not very many that connect marketing to the body as mine does. That's my "unique spin.")

ACTION STEP: *Your turn to brag.*

Journal through the following bragging prompts. Complete the ones that speak to you; then, complete the ones that challenge you. *I dare you!*

When answering the questions around the results that you deliver for your people—and the problems you solve—take special note: *These are the results your peeps aspire to. These are the problems your ideal clients are having right now.* Speak directly to their current challenge and where they want to be, and you will have their undivided attention.

BRAGGING PROMPTS

Here are some phrases to get you started owning your gifts. Whip out your journal and complete at least three of the following, three different ways:

Everywhere I go, I...

As a leader, this is what I bring to the table:

The secret of my success is...

I have a knack for...

My superpower is...

I don't normally brag about this, but I happen to be amazing at...

People who know me well say that what they love about me most is that I...

Because I experienced ________________, I learned _______________.

I have a degree from the School of Hard Knocks in ______________.

Malcolm Gladwell defines an "outlier" as someone who has gained mastery in an area through 10,000 hours or more of practice or experience.[23] *Looking back over my life, career and business, I have accumulated at least 10,000 hours doing this:*

My team works hard for me because I…

If I learned anything growing up, it's that…

If I learned anything as a <insert your role here>, it's that I…

What I could do all day gladly, with ease, is…

The thing I love to do more than anything is…

My peers recognize me for…

My favorite thing to do is…

What sets me apart from others in my field is that I…

I am proud of myself for…

I am most proud of the way I…

My top three achievements are…

---

[23] Gladwell, Malcolm. *Outliers: The story of success.* Little, Brown & Company (2008).

SISTERHOOD AMPLIFICATION: *Brag with other women.*

Practicing brags with other women is *where it's at.* That's where the rubber meets the road and you'll start to witness how women try to avoid bragging at all costs. (Talking about everything else, bragging about someone else while disguising it as a brag about themselves—I see women give credit for their work away all the time). You'll also notice the little "tells" that give away our discomfort and, you'll notice, water down the brag.

I spoke to a women's networking group just a couple weeks ago, and I took them through this exercise. We went around the room, taking turns bragging.

One woman candidly shared how she wasn't used to bragging, and didn't know what to say. (By the way, when you *least* feel like bragging is the *best* time to brag.)

Another woman, as she shared her brags, huffed her breath out in between brags, couching her brags with "I guess" and eye rolls and grimaces.

By the end, everyone was getting into it and lovingly "heckling" the bragger when she was, in truth, hiding.

The last woman to speak played off the previous woman's story, then launched into a story that actually bragged about the firm for which she was the communications coach. There were a whole lot of words… and no brag yet to be seen.

"Anyone notice what's missing?" I asked. Heads nodded enthusiastically and women piped in, encouraging her to brag about *herself* this time. It was a great, supportive group of ladies.

Now, *you* try bragging *out loud*, with a girlfriend, fellow entrepreneur or nonprofit leader, or in circle with a group of women you trust. Notice others' and your body language and verbal tics as you share your brags!

Bragging—celebrating our power and achievements—is a *practice*. The more you do it, the easier you'll find it to remember what you've accomplished, and fully own your beauty, intelligence and strength.

It is pleasure that connects a woman with her divinity and power.

—Regena Thomashauer

8

Clarify your desire

Connecting with your ideal client

The key to speaking directly to the heart of the people you serve is to know them so intimately, it's as if you speak the other side of a conversation they're already having in their heads.

You can only do this if you know them *really, really, really well*. And, if they can easily see themselves in your message.

The key to quickly and utterly getting your person's rapt attention is getting super-specific about who you serve. Like, niched-down, nitty-gritty-details super-specific.

Which almost always sends my clients into a tailspin.

We're afraid to get specific. To get exclusive.

Clarity and specificity, however, are *magnetic.*

I could hear Patty shift uncomfortably on the other end of the line. I was pressing her about her *ideal* client. "I'm a bookkeeper," she said. "I help everyone."

"You *can*, sure. But who are you *passionate* about serving?"

Silence. This was not language she used about her clients. I tried a different tack. "Who are your favorite clients?"

"Well, I work with a lot of contractors... Plumbers, handymen, construction folk. They work so hard all day, they don't have time to pay attention to their books, but a lot of money passes through their hands."

She was quick to add, "But I also help lawyers with their accounting... and I have one client who's an artist." Lawyers also work hard all day, don't have time to pay attention to their books, and a lot of money passes through their hands... but the pitch of her voice audibly flattened when she talked about them. Patty's voice was nearly surly when she talked about the artist, who it turned out was a total PITA (pain-in-the-ass) client referred by a close friend, so she felt obligated to help her, even though the artist was slow to get her the information she needed to do her job—and slow to pay, too.

We chatted a bit longer. I was helping Patty create a sales letter. The more we talked, the clearer it became: "You like the guys in trucks..." I announced, near the end of our call. "The guys who work with their hands; the guys in hard hats. *They are your people.*"

Patty was surprised. She didn't think she could get that specific with her clients—more than that, she hadn't believed that *her preferences* played any role in the ideal client equation. As the conversation came to a close, Patty said, "I learned more about my client in one conversation with you than in a year working with a marketing coach!"

Patty's sales letter spoke directly to the specific needs of her peeps, the guys in trucks. Why she admired them. What their unique pain points were, and what they aspired to achieve in their businesses. She could get super-specific because she got super-specific about who was on the receiving end of her message.[24]

We hesitate to get specific.

---

[24] See examples of the "love letter" approach to marketing on the Book Resources page at ShamelessMovement.com.

THE POWER OF SPECIFICITY

I don't want to exclude anyone.
Translation: If I say no to some people, then they won't like me.

Won't I miss out on business?
Translation: There's not enough business; if I miss out on this client, who knows when I'll get another? *If I lose this client, I won't make enough and we'll end up homeless and starving.*

I specialize in… [insert laundry list of services].
Translation: I do *everything*. And that other thing? Yep, I do that, too. Specialization *schmecialization.*

I'm a full-service…
(Stop!)

The less specific you are in staking a claim for the people you serve, the more you dilute your brand. How much *less* powerful would Patty's sales letter have been if she jumped around from contractors to lawyers to artists?

Conversely, if she truly had the passion to serve them all she could tailor a different sales letter to each client group—but likely there would be some other reason that her people were all her people, some commonality, like a shared social-mindedness, entrepreneurs who donate a portion of their proceeds or services, or work toward a purpose bigger than making a profit. This is a psychographic versus a demographic niche; either works, as long as you get specific, and get to know your niche market like a close friend.

The more specific you are, the more your audience feels that you are talking to them, and them alone. Think about the difference between getting an email that starts, "Hey guys," versus one that begins "Dearest reader." The first feels impersonal; the latter feels like the author sat down to write to you, personally—even though you are one of hundreds or thousands receiving the same message.

By being specific, you can address in detail the issues that obsess your client in particular. *The more you can use the actual language they use to describe their issues, the better.* And they'll give you that language, too: in the questions they constantly ask, in their testimonials, their description of why they started working with you, in their own words.

If you don't already have the words, *ask your clients*. Ask them why they started working with you. Ask how they felt and what challenges they were up against before working with you, and how they felt *after.* Ask why they switched from a "competitor."

Your clients' own words act like an irresistible aphrodisiac to prospects who align with your brand.

Unsure of who you prefer to work with? One of my business mentors, Fabienne Fredrickson says with a wry smile, "Serve 100 people. You'll know who you like and who you don't like."

If you've already served a number of clients, gather your notes on your top 5 all-time favorites. What do they have in common?

And if you still feel unsure, about planting your stake in the ground, *connect with your body* to sharpen your sense of what you like and what you don't. When we're excited to work with a particular client, *we can feel it.*

Try it. Think of one of your favorite clients right now, and notice the sensations in your body. Do you feel a surge of energy, does your heart beat a little faster, do you feel a pleasant warmth in your chest? Now think about a client that rubs you the wrong way. Do you feel your energy drop or flatten? Do your shoulders hunch forward slightly? Do you feel a constriction in your throat? Every body's cues will be different. They may be subtle—but the more often you tune in, the more you'll notice how clearly our body sends us messages and information, all the time.

THE POWER OF THE BODY: *Clarifying your true desire*

Why spend time discussing desire vis-à-vis your ideal client? Because so very often in creating their client avatar, my clients have considered everything *except* their own preferences. Time and again, it seems like *what* or *who* they love is irrelevant. I've made this mistake myself, taking on clients even when my intuition rang like a bell that we were not a good fit, or working on projects that, let's just say, didn't light my fire.

"Women are encouraged to and rewarded for taking a back seat to others' priorities. Putting everyone's needs ahead of her own," I wrote in *Every Day Pleasure*. Self-sacrifice meets with approval, while a woman directed by her pleasure is considered self-indulgent.

Because of this, we tolerate so much more than is necessary, including in our businesses. For example, crazy-making clients. If you hate any of your clients, if they are creating the opposite of pleasure in your life, *they're not your clients*. Let them go.

And if they're among your biggest clients, or you "need" them right now, take the steps required to replace them. One of my clients was terrified to fire her biggest customer; Samantha had a 6-figure business on account of this *one* client, a mid-sized business with a large sales team, who Samantha trained. But they made her miserable, running her at all hours. The owner was abusive when sales flagged, bellowing in her face.

"What can I do?" she fretted. This powerful woman who regularly ran top-notch trainings for national sales teams was near tears. She envisioned her family homeless and starving if she lost this account. I advised her to stockpile some cash, get her husband working again, get a bit of a safety net under her and then *let them go*. (Having jumped out of the nest *without* a safety net many times myself, I knew how quickly sheer terror could rubberband me right back into a not-so-great situation).

Samantha admitted that she already had three-months' savings in place. "But they're my whole business!" she protested.

"What does your body say?"

We were on day 2 of a weekend retreat I facilitated, so the question didn't come as a surprise. The whole retreat had been about tools for connecting with the body's wisdom. *Your body is your best business decision-making tool—a direct connection to your intuition*. She closed her eyes and got quiet.

A deep breath later, Samantha's eyelids fluttered open, her brow smooth and eyes clear. "I don't need them," she declared firmly. The other retreat participants cheered. She already seemed lighter at the idea of her business without this poisonous client.

Less than a month later, a partnership she was negotiating to keep her connection with this client alive fell through, and all ties were severed.

Less than two months later her revenue had rebounded. With her *yuck* customer gone, she actually had time to network and do what she does best: *sell.* When we last spoke, she had far surpassed her previous income.

By releasing a source of pain, *by honoring the importance of her own pleasure and experience,* Sam welcomed more business than she had been able to when sacrificing herself for the "good" of the client and their big fat checks.

The irony is that a woman directed by her pleasure is *irresistible*. Pleasure is fuel, guidance, her muse. Her wisdom. *A surefire cure to "stuckness" in your business or copy: spend some time in your pleasure—which means spending some time IN your body.*

THE POWER OF PLEASURE

A few years ago, I performed an experiment. I was the test subject, and the laboratory was my life.

Before my experiment, I had gotten so bogged down in the day-to-day grind, work-work-working without a break, I'd let my self-care fly out the window... Pleasure? *What pleasure?*

Tears started surprising me at incongruous moments, gently insisting that something was wrong. I had quietly slipped back into the all-too-familiar habits of a depression that characterized many of my adult years—and much of my childhood, too.

Like the frog in the pot, I didn't even feel the temperature of the water rising, the shift was so gradual.

I'd painted myself into a corner with work, obligations and a vision of the future that had less to do with "want" and more to do with "should."

Paralyzed by my blue mood, I felt like I was running. In place. In slow motion. I was desperate. I had to try something radical.

So I decided to do nothing but follow my pleasure, moment to moment, for a solid week. I danced and sweat, napped freely, and binged on videos by my heroines.

I wrote, expounding on what I love and detailing what I WANT. (It was so much easier to "hear" what that was when I focused on the little things that made me happy. I luxuriated in time with my children, my lover and the friends that kiss my soul.

As a divorced mother of two, running not one but two businesses, this was no easy feat. I felt resplendent... luxurious... and sometimes, a little guilty. Even a little nuts. *What am I doing?* I'd think. *I have so much to do!*

By the end of my intensive week of living playfully, I emerged totally nourished and fulfilled. When I sat at my desk, to projects over which I'd previously labored with little progress, *I completed them effortlessly*.

I had fed my inner muse, and she was eager and delighted to reward me.

I reaped immediate rewards in creativity, productivity and energy– and I was happy! I woke the morning of day five spontaneously smiling... When was the last time that had happened? I couldn't remember.

Pleasure is a practice. I'd learned this lesson many years before, vanquishing depression by turning ON to my life and following my pleasure, no matter how "selfish" it seemed. Taking my first bellydance class... beginning to perform... to teach... Pursuing it as a vocation.

What I realized from my experiment was that it takes vigilance. Tapping into our pleasure is not a one-time thing. It is an ongoing practice.

Pleasure requires daily practice. A week's sole-minded devotion to pleasure, to replenish a well that has run dry, is great... but not always possible, right?!

Daily small (and big) pleasures are necessary to keep the well filled.

To bring ourselves back into alignment with our happiness is a discipline. A daily discipline—of body, mind and spirit. [25]

ꕥ ꕥ

[25] Excerpted from *Every Day Pleasure,* in which I share 52 pleasure practices to sneak into your daily life—without adding to your to-do list. Access the rest of the book at ShamelessMovement.com/bookresources.

ACTION PLAN: 3 *daily rituals to re-friend the body*

How do you begin paying more attention to your body's messages... about *your* message? By getting back on speaking terms with her. Here are 3 ways to re-acquaint yourself with the source of your highest intelligence and guidance, your body.

The brain can discount words. But loving attention to the body through physical touch soaks into the cells, the brain.

To clarify, I am not prescribing yet another something to feel guilty about if you don't get to it every day. Take it easy. Do what speaks to you. You know your body best. (*Trust her*.)

1) Reclaim your morning shower.

Many of us rush through a shower with utilitarian fervor, getting in and out as quickly as possible. But how often do you have unencumbered time alone, naked and wet? This is an opportunity!

It doesn't need to be a long shower—though I do recommend slowing the pace of hand over skin. Enjoy the scent rising in the steam, the feel of water running over skin, your hands on your body. Savor the feel of skin on skin.

Put on a sexy tune and swivel your hips as you soap up and rinse. You may feel silly, *and that's even better*. This is about cracking open your pleasure, freedom and sense of play. Awakening your desire. In workshops, I lower the lights and we practice this tool to *Let's Get It On* by Marvin Gaye. Giggles abound. Yes! That's what I'm talking about.

Finally, don't compromise. Tune in to exactly what cleanser feels best on your skin, which smells refresh or bewitch you... This is not the place to skimp, nor does it need to be expensive. Just: EXACTLY what you want. Notice what you like, and what you don't like. And honor your tiniest desires around temperature, scent, and texture.

2) Anoint your body slower than slow.

Apply your post-shower moisturizer s-l-o-w-l-y... And then, go half that speed.

For extra credit: Witness your beauty. Get in front of the mirror and watch yourself.

The first time I did this, I saw my hand travel slowly down the length of a thigh I'd spent most of my life berating as "too big for shorts." I took in the graceful curve of my leg, the fine bones of my hand, the sensual drag of one over the other. Tears shook my shoulders.

Now, not a day goes by that I don't anoint some part of my body with frankincense, myrrh or sandalwood. What scents would you lovingly apply to your skin?

By slowing down and watching your reflection, you can no longer rush past appreciation.

3) Take a moment's pause... *and touch yourself*.

Physical touch grounds us as women.

That's right: *I'm telling you that touching yourself is a marketing tool*. And yes, you can touch yourself *wherever you like*. Lay a hand on belly, or cup hand over elbow, or rub the back of your neck in an impromptu self-massage. Give yourself a hug. Let your pleasure guide you.

If possible, enjoy the touch of skin to skin. Pleasure is our source—of power, information, comfort, love... Through touch, explore your body and your senses. As Mama Gena puts it: *Become a pleasure researcher*.[26] What areas of your body are most sensitive? What feels good?

---

[26] For more on the power of turn-on and pleasure research, read *Pussy: A Reclamation* by Regena Thomashauer, a/k/a Mama Gena.

Okay, I'm just going to put this out there, in case you didn't get my pussy-footing around the subject—*giggle*—or beating around the bush—*guffaw*:

Orgasm, for women, gets our creative juices flowing (pun intended) and grounds us in body and pleasure like no other experience. Just as it can restart a birthing mother's stalled labor, orgasm is a great way to get unstuck. Especially when you've reached a creative impasse, or aren't sure what you want, or have otherwise retreated from the wisdom of your body into trying to solve everything with only your brain. *Your turn-on is a great opener and teacher.*

(Yes, I am revealing this top-secret copywriter ninja-hack: *this tool busts through writer's block, no lie*.)

Which is part of why I recommend taking your "O-vitamins," daily.

How's THAT for shameless?

Savor your sensual shower. Moisturize slowly and deliberately. Pause and ground yourself with touch.... Even, and especially, "down there." Do this on the regular. And watch your appreciation for, and your connection to, your luscious body grow! [27]

Record your findings in your journal. What desires did you notice awakening in this practice?

SISTERHOOD AMPLIFICATION: *Hmm...*

No, I am not suggesting a group masturbatory experience. Unless of course that is your desire, in which case, *more power to you*. Rock on, sister.

You can do a little sister-sister activism: share this book or my Aspire article with a friend or colleague to try herself. (She can get her own copy at TheShamelessBook.com). Then compare notes!

---

[27] Adapted from a blog article I wrote for www.aspiremag.net, *Re-friending The Body: 3 Daily Rituals*.

Or as I described, "practice" any of these tools in circle with good girlfriends, like acting out your new morning shower, and have a good laugh besides!

Or when a girlfriend or colleague is stuck in a decision, ask this clarifying question: "What does your body say?"

And if you *really* want to disrupt the cobwebs from indecision, ask "What does your {*pussy*, or your preferred pet name for the center of your pleasure} say?"

Yep. Totally, utterly, *shameless.*

And undeniably powerful.

ꟻ ⅽ

Vulnerability is the birthplace of innovation, creativity and change.

— Brené Brown

9

Share your story

The power of vulnerability

Victoria and I met to discuss her messaging at a local fast food place. "Mainly, I need somewhere where my kids can run around while we talk," she explained. I.e., a play area with doors that lock. She had three plump-cheeked, round-nosed children, precocious and adorable; the youngest, still a newborn.

I asked who she serves in her business.

"Moms who want their kids to eat more fruits and veggies," she said. Yeah, *no.* My non-specific detector was going off. What she described is pretty much true of every mother, *ever*. We needed to narrow down who Victoria's ideal client was.

Victoria sells supplements that concentrate fruits and veggies into chewable form. Most of her messaging centered around the benefits of the product, how it had shortened the sniffles and otherwise halted the sickie "round-robin" that usually characterizes winter for families in our neck of the woods.

It wasn't a bad message; it just didn't strike a resounding emotional chord. Moms are constantly bombarded with marketing messages from companies, vying for their dollars, claiming to help them raise healthy kids. There is a lot of noise to cut through.

As her little ones roamed back and forth from play area to our table to dab French fries in ketchup and nibble, I asked how Victoria started her business. "It really began as I was looking for ways to keep my oldest healthy. He was sensitive to *everything*."

Victoria and her husband had found this out because her oldest was in and out of the hospital from the time he was born. For a while he was on goat's milk because it was the only thing he could keep down. Respiratory issues, digestive issues, his tiny body seemed to reject all substances. Fast forward a couple years and one of the few successful ways she had kept her little guy out of further hospitalizations and medical interventions were through these chewy supplements.

I stopped her right there. "Have you shared this story? The challenges you went through with your first baby?"

"Here and there," she replied. The bottom line was, she didn't *lead* with the compelling story of how she got started. Nor had she focused on moms coming from that very same place.

"Victoria, what if you targeted exactly that mom? Young moms who have tried everything to keep their little ones healthy, who are experiencing *now* what you experienced when your son was born. In and out of the hospital, feeling out of options, helpless, and as if the medical world had few answers to your questions." The challenges she faced, advocating for her son; the long commutes back and forth to NICU. These were details that her people could relate to, deeply.

It so happened that Victoria's compelling story—her *why*, the reason why she started her business, and why she's so passionate about it—was also a resounding clue as to *who* she could narrow her marketing down to meet.

Here is someone she knew intimately... An earlier version of herself.

EXPOSING THE VULNERABILITY MYTHS

Many business owners don't share their stories, because they're afraid of appearing unprofessional. Or the stories reflect a previous time so far removed from where they are now, like Vanessa's, that they've forgotten the visceral, emotionally charged reasons why they started down the entrepreneurial path.

Or, they're afraid that—should people know this detail about them—they would be rejected out of hand. My best friend Kim, who is literally one of the best resume writers in the world, hesitated to share that she started her writing business when she was driving a truck during the day to make ends meet. She wrote in the evenings and accessed Wi-Fi at truck stops to send and receive correspondence with her clients. She created resumes for executives and business leaders; what would they think of her if they knew the truth?[28]

Not surprisingly, her "backstory" is a part of what makes her so uniquely qualified to capture her clients' diverse backgrounds. The long drives gave her an opportunity to do the internal work of mulling over "just the right way to present her clients' experiences."

And most folks who hear about her trucker past think, like me, "How badass!"

One of our operating myths is that *vulnerability is weakness.*

Actually, to be vulnerable requires tremendous courage and strength.

Another myth is, *Don't let them see you sweat.* This is especially true for women. We're supposed to be able to balance a hundred spinning plates, but never appear as if we're exerting any effort. This myth is a prison of perfectionism.

---

[28] True story! She incorporated her origin story in her about page, beautifully. You can read all about her here: https://thislittlebrand.com/meet-kimberly/.

And yet, when you have heard someone else share a heartfelt story, or an experience that showed their humanity, did you feel drawn to them, or repelled?

The thing is, as so well put by Houston entrepreneur Gay Gaddis, "When you shut down vulnerability, you shut down opportunity."[29]

LET THEM SEE YOUR IMPERFECTION

I am a recovering perfectionist. What I've learned from overcoming the need to prove myself worthy at every turn is that in truth, our imperfection—our humanness—is an integral part of our appeal to our tribe.

When Fabienne Fredrickson recorded a video to send to her mailing list, announcing a livestream of an upcoming event, halfway through, her youngest son started crying and screaming in the background. She acknowledged him, kept rolling, finished her message, assuring the audience with a laugh, "Don't worry, the event will be less chaotic than what's happening right now." She had a choice: to start over and re-record the video, or share it *as-is*. She went with the riskier, more vulnerable choice—complete with her then walking over to comfort her little one while her oldest played with the ball he'd wanted.[30] She later shared that so many clients, when signing up for her program, said that it was *this video* that showed them that she was the business coach for them: she was a real business owner and a real mom. In other words, she was *just like them.*

HOW MUCH IS TOO MUCH? *How to know what to share*

People are often afraid of sharing too much, or the wrong story.

---

[29] Full article here: ShamelessMovement.com/bookresources

[30] Ditto above to see the video.

A simple guideline I offer is this: ask yourself *why* you want to share a particular story. "Is this for me alone, or will it serve the greater good?"

Is it a *relevant* story for your people? Will it help them relate to you, or does it provide a "teachable moment?"

Mine your past experiences for gifts.

Stories are how we connect with each other—and the stories that demonstrate our passion, our why, our truth, even more so.

As for the stories that we hide: the closer we hold them, the more power they have over us.

ACTION STEP: Your compelling story.

Now it's your turn. What is your compelling story? Why did you start your business? Why do you do the work that you do? What drives you?

Sometimes, like my friend the resume writer, it's not a story that has to do with the inception of your business but a certain something that—contrary to your belief that you must hide this aspect of yourself—makes you more appealing to the very people you want to reach. (For example, I'm a speaker who is also a copywriter who is also a bellydancer. I could keep those worlds separate, but—believe it or not, my ideal clients overlap across these spaces.)

Could you pull back the curtain and reveal some of your past or present "messiness"? How being a mother influences your business? How you handled a health crisis and kept your business afloat—or allowed yourself a compassionate hiatus?

Are you sitting on a story that your potential clients would love to know—that would let them know that you're human too, that you've been where they've been?

It's time to tell that story.

SISTERHOOD AMPLIFICATION:

There is the telling of the story... and then there is the being witnessed in the telling of it. We need to be witnessed, as human beings. And: shame evaporates on exposure. It can only exist shrouded in secrecy.

Call up a close friend who you know will hold you in a space of total non-judgment and receptivity. Ask if they are willing to listen, then read them your compelling story.

Not sure who to call? Record a video or audio and post it (unlisted) on YouTube, then email me the link at shamelessauthor@gmail.com. It is my honor to witness you.

As we learn to bear the intimacy of scrutiny, and to flourish within it, as we learn to use the products of that scrutiny for power within our living, those fears which rule our lives and form our silences begin to lose their control over us.

— Audre Lorde

10

Embrace the shadow

A word of anticipation

You'll know you're doing something right when...

I had just finished a solo performance at a benefit. My gold dress clung to my body like a second skin, and I had done what I do best—wooing the audience, spinning around the stage, *being myself*. As I stepped off the dance floor, the dancer up next threw a comment out of the corner of her mouth.

"Well, that was cute."

Did I imagine a hint of a sneer in her voice? My eyebrows raised and I kept walking to the "dressing room," the dry good storage area of the restaurant where we were performing. Mirrors were propped on huge cans of crushed tomatoes and hangers dangled from shelves storing napkins and silverware. (Ah, the glamorous life of a bellydancer!)

Inwardly, I chuckled. *I think I just got my first catty comment!* I thought to myself. A performer's rite of passage.

It was not to be the last. Another time, I taught a choreography by a popular dancer to my students. It was a brilliant mix of silken fluidity and percussive hips. We performed the dance for its creator. We danced, the audience applauded, she smiled.

Backstage as I peeled off my costume, I watched as a prominent figure in the local dance community solemnly applied make-up to one of her students, preparing for an upcoming number. Without looking up from her task, she said severely, “Don’t you *ever* perform that song again.”

Without a mirror, I knew my mouth was in a perfect “o” of astonishment.

In the world of Oriental dance, it is not uncommon to run into questions of authenticity and misappropriate cultural references. The rhythms in the music I had just danced to were similar to rhythms used in the *zar,* a ritual dance where women gather and release their demons—emotional, physical, psychological, or real—through repetitive trance-like movements. It is a transcendent experience that I have since been fortunate to participate in.

At the time, I didn’t know what to say. Afterward, I thought, *Heyyyyy, I didn’t ask your opinion*. But as a woman of color, descended from a culture oft-colonized and pillaged by invaders, I am sensitive to cultural appropriation, so I apologized.

Later, as I learned more about Egyptian music and culture I learned that *context is everything*. The rhythm may have been the same but instrumentation, arrangement, everything else in the music said “not ritual.” In the same way that performers have evolved *tanoura,* a secular version of Sufi spinning—a religious ceremony—by changing the costuming (colorful, even decorated with LED lights) versus the traditional (neutral garb). All the cues say “not ritual,” making it okay for non-Sufis to perform it as a folk dance.

The most intense reaction I ever received as a dancer was when I again followed a fluid, demure dance with a more raucous, “street dance” style. (Femininity comes in more than one flavor.) A dancer in the audience said, “You started out so beautiful! But when you got to that part…” I had jumped up on chairs and danced, and moved close to the patrons who sat at scattered cocktail tables.

“I was so mad I wanted to punch you in the face,” she finished.

All this to say: *Expect backlash.*

The more you show up, the more people will feel free to tell you exactly what they think of you.

In an interview, Nina Simone described how interesting she found the way people responded to *Four Women.* The iconic song tells the story of four generations/archetypes of African American women: Aunt Sarah, a slave and elder, beaten and disrespected; Saffronia, the light-skinned child of rape; Sweet Thing, who sells the curves of her body; and Peaches, bitter and angry.[31]

The responses were as diverse as the women themselves—some people thought Sweet Thing was a poor representative of African American womanhood; others thought Peaches too angry. Some were hurt by the reference to rape. Simone chuckles in the interview at the variety and passion of response. She was someone who could give a *Mississippi Goddam* about what people think of her.

Then she said something that I never forgot, even though I can't find the interview now to save my life—I believe it's from an original LP of hers. "That is the role of the artist," she stated. "*To incite a response.* I cannot control what that response is, or *how* the audience responds. My sole duty, however, is to *incite* the response. To speak to the most important issues of my day. That is the job of the artist."

Her words speak in many ways to my thoughts on leadership. *It is our job to challenge the status quo, to incite response, to spark change.* And, it means that not everyone will be a fan.

The brighter you shine your light, the greater the darkness will encroach. The more you stir the pot, the more you will get feedback both positive and negative[32].

---

[31] See the incomparable Nina Simone performing *Four Women*, and a powerful modern treatment of the song, here: ShamelessMovement.com/bookresources

[32] A great example of the onslaught that we face in the modern age of faceless online commentary is the UnderArmour commercial featuring model Gisele, here: ShamelessMovement.com/bookresources

On the other side of playing big is getting a whole 'lot more attention.

So… prepare yourself. *And welcome it.*

Lips parted, a smile playing across them; torso expanded and open; shoulders thrown back; belly, soft. *Bring it.*

You know you're doing something right…

Sometimes, often, the biggest resistance will come not from external sources, but internally. But now you have tools, resources. Check in with the body; douse yourself with pleasure. See how loud the internal criticism or negative self-talk is after you've basked in some self-care.

(Exquisite self-care is not a luxury for the modern-day woman leader—it is required sustenance, especially and even more so if you are here to do big work.)

ACTION STEP: *Feel the backlash.*

Where have you already experienced backlash for showing up bigger or brighter? Externally or internally. Take a few minutes to journal the story. If the memory pangs you, take a few more minutes to consider the story with this new frame—as fuel, not reason to stop or shut down.

Reframe the story: rewrite the criticism or negative response as a sign that you're on the right path. We *want* people to unsubscribe from our lists if they find what we have to say offensive or boring or unrelatable. If they do, *they're not our people*. Love them and set them free.

If critics or naysayers hit a tender spot with you, it's okay. Feel the feelings, and *move* through them. Feel the anger and stomp around to a rage-y song. Some of my favorite angry dance songs, each with its own vibe and nuance, are *Counting Bodies Like Sheep to the Rhythm of the War Drums*, by eMOTIVe, *You Oughta Know* by Alanis Morrissette, and *Piece of My Heart* by Janis Joplin. Pound a pillow, let yourself grunt and yell. Let your anger move!

If you feel sad because maybe your detractors are echoing a secret judgment or belief you have about yourself, that's okay too. (Often there's grief behind the rage). Drop to your knees, roll around on the floor, fully feel and express the feelings. My all-time favorite songs that go right to my sad, wallow place is *This Woman's Work* by Kate Bush, *Station* by Låpsley, and *Pray You Catch Me* by Beyoncé. Let the tears flow, let your voice wail, ball your fists in your hair, shake your head, curl and open your body.

Whatever the feeling, find the song that helps you "go there" and let your body lead the way. (She'll know what to do.)

The critical next step—program these songs next on your playlist—is to follow up your emotion-dancing songs with music that will move you into a creative, sensual place. (Don't skip this step and head straight for the shiny-happy songs... it will disrupt the process. This is about feeling the feelings, not bypassing them.)

Why creative, sensual place? Remember what I said about pleasure? This is the state where we create and attract, effortlessly. Naturally. It is part of our magic as women. We tap it when we let our bodies begin to unleash, to be their freed, sexy selves. On my sensual playlist, my transition from my deep, "swampy" songs to my happy place, are songs like: *Feelin' Love* by Paula Cole, *6 Inch* by Beyoncé, *Pony* by Ginuwine, and *Let's Get It On* by Marvin Gaye. You get the idea![33]

Finally, if you want to ramp up your energy and end on a high note (if you're not already there!), end your playlist with a sunny song that always gets your feet tapping and raises your vibration. I have so many of these but a few of my favorites are *Happy* by Pharrell Williams, *I Love Me* by Meghan Trainor, *What'd I Say* by Maceo Parker, and *Signed, Sealed, Delivered* by Stevie Wonder.

How we respond to our critics and detractors, how we handle the backlash—even and especially our own internal damning voices—is an integral part of visibility.

SISTERHOOD POWER-UP: *Share the love.*

Spread more light. Who do you admire? Who inspires you? Who are you grateful for? Send them a thank you card. A bouquet of flowers. A tribute. A poem. Counteract backlash by "forwardlashing" appreciation.

EXTRA CREDIT: *Gather the praise.*

Put all the praise, testimonials, kind emails, and thank you cards from people you've impacted and put them all in one place—a folder on

---

[33] This exercise is inspired by the "swamping" practice from the School of Womanly Arts, as described in Regena Thomashauer's book, *Pussy: A Reclamation.* Having "swamped" in a room with hundreds of other women, what I can tell you is that it is a powerful practice that more than once has kept me grounded in times of crisis. I share a video showing you how to swamp on the Book Resources page at ShamelessMovement.com.

your computer, a beautiful box or container—and when the backlash is especially harsh, read through your collection. It will remind you that your purpose is bigger than any criticism, self- or otherwise. Ultimately, it's not about you, but the people you serve, and continuing to increase and enrich your impact.

ꙮ

Who is the Wild Woman?

She is the incubator. She is intuition, she is far-seer, she is deep listener, she is loyal heart. She encourages humans to remain fluent in the languages of dreams, passion, and poetry.

She is ideas, feelings, urges, and memory. She has been lost and half forgotten for a long, long time. She is the source, the light, the night, the dark, and daybreak. She is the smell of good mud and the back leg of the fox.

She is the voice that says, "This way, this way."

— Dr. Clarissa Pinkola Estés

11

This is what shameless looks like

Next steps

As I cautioned at the outset: *this is not a one-and-done process*.

Embracing our shadow, developing what Brené Brown calls "shame resilience" is ongoing work.

The results of the work are undeniable:

Visibility without shame or apology.

Confidence in your message, because it resonates deeply with your purpose and intuition as communicated through your most loyal consort, your body.

No more fear of competition—because with no one like you on the planet, and in all of time, you can safely say *you have no competition.*

Expansive, positive expectation.

Increased impact: by showing up bigger, you gain more *aligned* clients, more sales, more job offers, and greater visibility of your cause and organization.

Freedom. From binding stories, from limiting beliefs... Freedom to act as your authentic, most powerful self.

Freed energy, wisdom and healing—that have been with you all along.

It has been my honor to share this process and journey with you—and know too, that we have only just scratched the surface. The stories will continue to come up—especially the bigger and brighter you shine. The bigger the front, the bigger the back; the bigger the goal, the louder resistance will clamor.

And now you have tools to reconnect with your body's intelligence and your authentic story, and oust shame from the driver's seat.

ACTION STEP: *Ask for help.*

You *can* do it alone... *Or we can do it together*. In community. In sisterhood. To amplify, and accelerate your results. Let's go deeper. *The world needs you*.

If you would like to learn more about doing this work, one-on-one or in circle with other passionate, purpose-driven women entrepreneurs, these are exactly the yummy women I gather. You can check out a what we're all about at ShamelessMovement.com.

Bring your stories, bring your brags, bring your beautiful body, and *let's do this*.

SISTERHOOD AMPLIFICATION: Pay it forward.

If you received value from this work, I would be so honored if you share it. Pass your copy of this book on, or send friends and colleagues to get their own copy at: ShamelessMovement.com/book.

Open your heart, fling your hopes high and set your dreams aloft. I am here to hold your hand.

—Maya Angelou

Afterword

Where do we go from here?

The very creation and publication of this book has taken me through my own struggle with visibility. (*No way*, right? Ha.)

I wrote the first draft in March of 2018. Over 100 pages came flowing out in a whoosh—or, as my friend Kim likes to say, "You pooped it out in three weeks." This book is a culmination of material about which I have taught, written, researched, and lived, for years.

I bought the ISBN, uploaded it to (then) Amazon's self-publishing platform, Createspace. I ordered proofs, and gave all but one away.

And then, I proceeded to sit on the book, for the next year. Promising a launch that never happened. I edited it, for sure, in fits and starts. But its public, to-the-world, available-for-purchase launch kept getting pushed further and further off.

I knew this book would take me to a new level of visibility... It exposes some of my deeply held truths and very private stories. It would not be everyone's cup of tea. And I was scared.

Would I be judged? Would people still like me? Would they laugh at me? Or worse, would they dismiss me?

In the end, it's not about me. Yes, these concepts and tools have helped me overcome a debilitating fear of being myself, authentically, for all the world to see. The results of which, so far, have been... astounding. I freed myself from a first marriage that worked for no one. I became a nationally award-winning bellydancer. I grew a freelance writing side hustle into a six-figure (and counting) copy agency with a team of writers and support staff. And with this book, I launch the Shameless Movement.

And: You and I, we're the same. I may be a few steps up the path from you in some regards, and not in other ways—but we are no different. I share my message with you in the hope that it helps you to share your message with the world. Because *the world needs you*. You were called, as I was, at this moment in time, at this point in history, in this place. You, like me, are unlike anyone else who has or will walk the planet.

And if, like me, you feel disappointed, frustrated, some kind of way about delaying your visibility—let that go. Our timing is perfect and elegant.

Through every iteration of this book, I never quite felt satisfied with the ending. There was a piece missing.

I begin with the epic story of an ancient ritual, the traditional Egyptian wedding march that echoes other ceremonies like it, where woman transmutes energy to transform, her body a conduit for creation. In that instance, she changes a girl to woman in time for her wedding night, simply by virtue of her presence.

Not altogether different from pregnancy, where woman stewards fertilized egg from conception to new life, her body the vessel as soul focuses into flesh.

And that is where I found myself, just a few months ago.

Despite a few silver hairs, and an age that would prompt conventional medicine to deem my pregnancy "geriatric," my husband and I were expecting a child—his first, my third. (By the way, any woman over 35 who conceives is considered to have a "geriatric" pregnancy... Ridiculous, that that line of demarcation hasn't been updated despite the fact that we are living longer, healthier lives, not to mention that aging is a mindset—just ask Dr. Christiane Northrup.[34] *But I digress.*)

My period was only late by a few weeks when I bought the pregnancy test, but the signs were unmistakable. When I was pregnant with my second child, I knew the instant she was conceived; she fluttered like a butterfly in the womb. My then-husband scoffed when I declared myself pregnant, but, well... you know who won that argument.

This little one felt different, more like she was dog-paddling around in there, flipping over and back, like a miniature dolphin with legs. There were external clues, too: the boob fairy had arrived. My current husband, Marcin, was googly-eyed with admiration. So, we had our suspicions, but it was too soon to confirm.

I hid the test under the bathroom sink, planning to perform the ceremonial peeing-on-the-stick on Christmas morning. The holiday arrived, and it was well before dawn when I snuck out of bed to take the

---

[34] Northrup, Christiane, M.D. *Goddesses Never Age: The Secret Prescription for Radiance, Vitality and Well-Being.* Hay House, Inc. (2015) Author of the iconic *Women's Bodies, Women's Wisdom,* Dr. Northrup wrote *Goddesses* more recently. In it, she relates how, as a longtime obstetrician and gynecologist, she had been struck that despite every one else's cooperation with the idea that the older you are, the more difficult it is to conceive and birth a baby, she found the opposite in the Irish Catholic community she served in Boston, Massachusetts in the late 70s/early 80s. Within that community, women were told from the time that they were girls that they were extremely fertile and could get pregnant at the drop of a hat. Combine that belief with the cultural expectation to do just that—pop out babies as often and as long as humanly possible—and the mothers that Dr. Northrup supported continued to get pregnant well into their 50s with no issue. She quipped that the only way she could get the women to *stop* conceiving, in those instances where the mother's health as at risk, was to tie their tubes!

pregnancy test, since I still had loads to do before the rest of the household woke. (I am notorious for shopping for gifts in the last days before Christmas... More than one Eve found me, kids in tow, at Toys R Us, back when that was still a thing. So, needless to say, I still had to wrap everything.)

I followed the stick's teeny print instructions. The little window in the stick immediately showed pregnant, the lines vivid; no vague faded lines here.

My early training as a scientist, however, means that I follow protocol. (To this day, when measuring any liquid, I add and pour out until the bottom of the liquid's meniscus aligns with the measuring line for, say, 10 cc's of silver hydrosol or three cups of vegetable stock).

I waited the requisite two minutes to confirm that the results didn't change. At two minutes, 3 seconds, I straddled Marcin's sleeping form and nudged him awake. I whispered in his year. "Merry Christmas, Daddy," and watched as he groggily processed what I'd said. It took a few repetitions before the import of my words registered. And to think that, just the night before, in a Polish tradition that Marcin's family follows every year, we exchanged our blessings for the year with each person, one by one. My sister-in-law, after wishing for me the usual—health, prosperity, good times—added with a mischievous wiggle of her brow, "And maybe... something else? You know? A little something new?" She hinted playfully around adding a family member. *If only she knew!* I thought, but resisted the urge to break the news before its time.

The next six weeks progressed as expected. I became fuller, rounded, with the extra blood flow, amniotic fluid, the placenta. Yep, I glowed. The little, winnowy movements of Little One became more pronounced. It was still well ahead of when I was "supposed" to feel anything, but she made her presence felt. And she was definitely a *she,* I intuited, although I tried not to assign any pronouns.

I had already told my innermost circle about my pregnancy, and started to share the news with the next ring of contacts, individually, when it felt natural to do so. My journal held sketches of a pregnant woman, rounded with a little lima bean fetus curved in her womb; and the tree of life, which mimics the web of blood vessels that connect mother to placenta.[35]

It was early February. My last period had been in November. As if waking from a dreamlike state, I suddenly had the thought, *Gee whiz, I need a midwife!* I Googled and found one not 30 minutes from my house. Also, I had started spotting, which worried me, and reminded me that this is exactly the kind of question for a birth caregiver.

To be honest, I was more than a little worried. My bestie Kim reassured me, "It's totally normal. I bled with my oldest, like bled as if I was on my period bled, and it was fine." I clung to her words.

But. But I had woken a couple days prior feeling *not pregnant*. The rich, buzzing fullness of pregnancy was gone and my body felt... deflated. Un-animated. I could no longer sense the presence of my daughter, who had been a constant, alive, fluttering presence up until then.

Just the week before, I had been in Connecticut, receiving a session from Carrie, a myofascial release genius from the UK. As my body melted under her hands, inexplicably, I remembered a story told of Hawaii, that pregnant women travel to the islands to birth their babies in the ocean with the dolphins. An acquaintance's wife had actually steered their moving to the big island because of her overwhelming determination to birth there. Intending to stay only for their firstborn's arrival and a little recover time, years later, they were still residents. He said, remembering, "As soon as my feet touched the ground after we got off the plane, I knew we were home."

Little One leapt and swirled and kicked her little limbs as I thought of swimming with the dolphins. Carrie later gushed reverently, "When my hands were on either side of your womb," one hand atop abdomen, the other at lower back, "it felt as if I was holding the Universe."

When I returned to Illinois and researched the actual practice of birthing with the dolphins, I thrilled to the photos of rounded mamas

---

[35] For reals. Google placenta and tree of life and you'll find tons of examples, or go to the resource page at: ShamelessMovement.com/bookresources

swimming with the beautiful creatures in the blue, blue ocean. But when I clicked to the page showing a woman, her swollen belly vulnerable, surrounded by dolphin "midwives," my whole body was like, *Oh, hell no*. I'll keep my bare feet on the ground while a human midwife catches my baby in the comfort of my own home, thank you very much. Hence, my quest for a local midwife.

We met with Bonnie, the midwife, for our initial consultation in her living room. The room was immaculate, the house like a cabin in a New England wood, or maybe I imagined that since Bonnie's pleasant yet reserved and crisp demeanor reminded me of Maine. She said that she usually starts working with mommas earlier in their pregnancy, but since I had birthed before and at home with my second, she wasn't concerned. I learned later that had I not birthed my daughter at home, proving that I could successfully have a VBAC (vaginal birth after Cesarean), Bonnie never would have taken me as a client.

She didn't blink twice at my 40+ age. I loved her for that.

I waited patiently, until formalities were complete. Finally, I could hop on Bonnie's table so she could take a listen to Little One. She had a crackling, older-model ultrasound unit. She jellied up my abdomen and rooted around its surface with the smooth, handheld doppler, tucking in here, then there. Pressing into the womb, then deeper still, listening for the baby's heartbeat. I had already informed her of the spotting, and she, like Kim, had reassured me.

The machine was quiet. She probed some more. Minutes passed, and I resisted the wave of dread hovering just beyond my field of sight. Bonnie was quick to comfort me, "It's still a little early to hear the heartbeat with this machine. They'll have more advanced technology at the hospital, where we can confirm the baby's heartbeat. It happens all the time, they can hear what this one can't."

She wrote a referral for an ultrasound. It was dark when we left Bonnie's. I called the local hospital and was able to get scheduled for the next afternoon.

I woke the next morning to more blood, gobs of it. A sob wrenched from my throat. In the bathroom, I squeezed the towel rack in my hands, head bending to touch forehead to the coarse nap of the towel that hung there. "Please, Divine Mother," I prayed as tears squeezed past shut-tight eyelids. "Please, oh God..."

My life has been a string of polarities, of circumstances and experiences, impossibly contained within a single lifetime: bellydancer and accountant; writer and neuroscientist; chemist and musician. Cesarean and home birth. Corporate employee and entrepreneur. As a mixed race person, Filipino and German, I've experienced racism and privilege both. Inner city schools and private liberal arts college. Life below and above the poverty line. Physical abuse. Travel across 4 continents. Sexual harassment. An emotionally abusive marriage with an unfaithful husband. Divorce. Remarriage. Childbirth. My running interpretation is that I've experienced all this so I can be a more effective writer and teacher, relate to and connect with even more people.

I whispered, begging All That Is, "I don't need to experience this, too."

On my way to the hospital, not one but two hawks swooped overhead. In a clearing to my left, I spotted a group of deer, heads bobbing from nibbling at the undergrowth poking up through the snow to vigilant scanning for predators. My mouth formed an O as I saw there were double the number among the bare trees just past them—more deer than I'd ever seen gathered at once, does with their fawns. I turned my attention back to the road, reeling with the hushed magic of the moment.

At last I arrived at the hospital. A technician ushered me to radiology, then left as I undressed, then slipped into a hospital gown and under a sheet in the dimly-lit room. The technician returned and asked if I'd ever had an internal ultrasound before. I breathed as she pressed a wand inside me, sweeping it at different, not always comfortable angles. We listened. Waited. Nothing.

She continued to scan while I strained to hear the familiar, rapid *whoosh-whoosh-whoosh*.

"I'm not finding a heartbeat," the technician said finally, her eyes compassionate.

"What do we do now?" I asked, stunned.

She didn't answer. "I am so sorry. Do you want to see her?"

"She is a her?"

"Yes, definitely." She probed around, showing me her small form as it emerged on the screen. Even though I was 11 weeks along, Little One was as small as a 7- or 8-week old. From one angle she looked like a tiny dolphin, still and silent against my uterine wall.

The hopeful suspension of disbelief of the previous few days suddenly cleared, as neurons fired to connect the dots. It occurred to me what the letters on Bonnie's referral had meant: ultrasound for possible SA. *Spontaneous abortion*, the medical term for miscarriage. I realized abruptly, *there are no further tests.* No heartbeat here means... there is no heartbeat. She was gone.

I stood to prepare to leave, and my hands flew of their own accord to my face. "I knew it, I knew something was wrong!" The tears came, hot and sudden. The technician hugged me tight, awkward around my folded arms. And I loved her for that.

In the car, I called my husband, then Kim, reporting the news; then cried until I could see straight again. The deer were exactly where I left them, grazing peacefully. Nothing had actually changed.

Bonnie talked me through what to expect next with her kind, matter-of-fact pragmatism. "One in four pregnancies ends in miscarriage. It just happens," she comforted me. "It's not your fault, you didn't do anything wrong."

My friend Marie had been calling and texting all day. "What happened? You are so in my head! What is going on?" I finally called her the next day, telling her the whole story as she held space for me. She kept me company as the cramps increased, reaching a climax. We ended our call, and a moment later there was intense pressure, then I felt the baby pop through my cervix. I called downstairs to Marcin who came and knelt at my side, on the tiled floor of our bathroom. He held my hand as I leaned into his shoulder. We bowed our heads and wept together. It was one of the few times I had seen him cry. It felt like we were children, praying.

A month passed. The grief had dulled somewhat; I no longer cried every day. Life's rhythms had thrummed back to their daily drum. Person by person, I had to un-announce the baby. I hated seeing their faces change from joyful "How are you *feeling?*" to sad "Oh honey, I'm so sorry."

I flew into Boston to visit with Marie before heading on to Connecticut for business. She picked me up and drove me out to her 100+ year-old farm. It was the first I'd seen it. A huge black dog guided me from the car to the front door, tail wagging over snow- and ice-covered mud.

Marie settled me in a room at the cap of stairs hollowed by generations of foot traffic. She fed me spinach and farm-fresh eggs, coffee with raw milk and addictive seed crisps. She took one look at my knit Uggs and shook her head. "Those aren't going to cut it." I borrowed a pair of her husband's rubber muck boots that hugged my calves.

"We're doing ceremony," Marie announced. "I planned to do it tomorrow, but my guides are saying now, today." She outfitted me with a full skirt to wear over my jeans, and oversized hooded sweatshirt hand painted with feathers. "Do you have a hat? Gloves? We're going to be out there for a while."

In my own gloves and borrowed woolen hat, we headed outside. We tromped past rabbits, goats, horses and cows, boots crunching through the top layer of frozen snow. Past pond and outbuildings and finally on a winding, narrow trail into the woods. As we passed a big black rock marked with a short cairn of white stones, Marie said cryptically, "Walk around that; be careful not to touch it."

We arrived at a small clearing amid the trees. Sacred items marked each direction. Much of the medicine wheel was buried in the snow. We rolled out our yoga mats, fuchsia and blue against the white, something to protect our rear ends from the frozen ground; wrapped ourselves up in blankets against the cold; and began. After smudging, praying and offering tobacco to our guides and ancestors, Marie began to drum. She walked me through what to listen for, to know when to return, and we fell into deep meditation as the rhythm tethered us to the earth.

Here was my vision:

I was taken to a green expanse of field, my entry point marked by a great tree. In the branches of the tree were oval globes of clear smooth crystal that sparkled. Beyond the tree, lining the field, I saw the long wall of a gray stone castle; its length was studded with a row of narrow windows that arched nearly the height of the building.

Through glass panes clouded with age, I saw at the center of the great hall, a beautiful older woman with white-gold hair. It was my daughter, Little One. She sat at the head of a long banquet table peopled with creatures, human and not. It was as if they had stepped, 3-dimensional, from cave paintings. A fire burned in a huge hearth on the opposite wall. The long table was old and dusty, laden with platters of food from a long-ago feast.

My daughter wore a gown of blue velvet, squared at the neckline; it draped from her shoulders, falling behind her in a swath of fabric.

Then I was in the banquet hall with her. I lay my head on her shoulder, as we fell in step together, side by side, clasping hands. Her shoulder and gown were soft but her hand was hard and gnarled—at first, I thought bone, but no, it was more like holding hands with the fine, dry branch of a tree, warmed by the sun.

As we walked, she let it be known to me that she had been my mother in prior lifetimes. I cried, feeling the truth of it. We continued strolling on the castle grounds, past a low stone wall into a copse of closely-grown trees, their branches bare.

We knelt at a brook that crossed our path. I saw her reflection beside me, but where my face should be, there was nothing—a hollow loop, like some angel sculptures I've seen. And then, I *was* the water.

Cool and lithe, I slipped over the rocks and around bends, glittering in the sunshine. I emerged downstream, again a woman, but only half; my legs were a deer's. My breasts were big and pendulous; my belly, pregnant. My legs wobbled, shaking the water beading and rolling off my fur; my hooves beat against the flat gray rock. I continued walking with my queen mother.

She came to stand behind me and held my breasts, offering them to creatures who also began to emerge from the water, some human, some not. I recognized them from the banquet table. They came to suckle at my breasts.

At first I resisted, I wasn't sure I wanted to, and then Sacred Wind, my mother, my daughter, took me on her lap and held me. Cradling and comforting me, I was like an infant nursing in her arms. I no longer felt afraid to suckle the beings that came because I, too, was fed. I felt safe.

While in her arms, I went into labor. One by one, without pain or effort, from between the folds of my vulva I birthed luminescent, translucent, perfectly oval crystals, the size of ostrich eggs. They emerged, one after another, aglow and pearlescent. Light babies.

Marie's drum began to call me back. The stream had become an ocean, and my mother-daughter and I walked toward it.

The drum quickened, insistent. Sacred Wind took the blue mantle from her shoulders and placed it on mine. I felt the weight of the fabric falling behind me.

In my right hand, she placed a scepter.

And on my head she placed a tall crown of antlers.

Silhouetted against the sky, I walked toward the horizon, the call of the drum and Marie at the medicine wheel.

You don't need to be the wedding dancer or go on a vision quest to know what medicine you bring to the planet.

It may be a dream you've had since you were a child, a passion that has emerged over the course of your life, or a something tied to a skill that comes so easy to you, you've never given it a second thought.

Your medicine calls through the tears that well up when you think about a certain something, the righteous anger that bubbles over when you consider a person's, animal's or environment's plight.

It calls by the simple joy and ease you feel in your body when you're acting *in* your purpose.

The call can be delivered by your ancestors, as to Marie, through clear instructions – or a gentle tug every time you drive past the homeless shelter on the way home.

Whatever your calling is, you will know it by the way that it is bigger than you. The way it scares you a little bit. The way it demands that you stretch, reach, and be your best self.

What mantle of leadership has been passed to your shoulders?

Sisters, we have been called, we have returned, at this moment of time, very much on purpose: to swing the pendulum back. Not from patriarchy to matriarchy but to a renewed, balanced world that reveres and honors both feminine and masculine, yin and yang, spirit and body. A regal buck's antlers as well as the blue robes of the Sacred Mother.

Together we are here to build a world that, in fact, rejects simplistic polarities like these to embrace diverse perspectives, a place in the circle for all peoples. To build a community that loves and honors the planet, its elders, its children, and all of its residents.

Hierarchy is *so* last millennium.

This is the way of women's wisdom, of queen's leadership, *in circle*. And we cannot bring our medicine to the world without bringing our whole selves in, without shame, without apology.

(This is not the time for the hokey pokey: *I put my left foot in, and my right shoulder, and shake them all about—but not my jiggly bits or that thing that happened to me when I was seventeen*.)

The world we are co-creating, my sister, requires *all* of you. All of your brilliance, every beloved cell of you, all of your devastating experience and skill. We would not be complete without you. You, in your whole shameless genius.

I am so honored and delighted to dance with you, at this point in time, at this place, whenever and wherever this book lands in your hands. Thank you for walking this path with me.

As I close every women's circle, I leave you with these words:

From my heart to yours,

I love you.

Take what you need and pass it on.

Further Resources

I could easily fill another book with the wonderful resources and inspirations that inform my work and that will broaden and deepen your understanding of the topics covered in this book. Here is a list of some of my favorites; it is by no means exhaustive! Let your pleasure and curiosity guide you to find your own, and share them with your sisters—and with me, on the Shameless Movement Facebook page.

The Shameless Movement

Welcome, beloved! The culmination of years of study and offerings, the Shameless Movement is a support system and springboard for the woman boldly embracing her Queendom.

A combination of online and in-person experiences that immerse you in tools and community, it includes what you learned in this book and beyond... So you may accelerate and amplify your impact, to lead and love as only you can.

Joining the Shameless Movement is free. Simply check out our website at TheShamelessMovement.com to begin your journey.

Browse around my blog. Sign up for love letters, pockets of *Shameless* inspiration and wisdom delivered to your inbox. Learn about our courses and community offerings, and join the movement!

And of course, find additional resources mentioned in the book at shamelessmovement.com/bookresources.

Community

Share your insights on the Shameless Movement Facebook page: www.facebook.com/ShamelessMovement

Join the Facebook group at
www.facebook.com/groups/shamelessmovement

Books by *moi*

Every Day Pleasure: A bellydancer's perspective on how to add more time, more fun & more passion, daily.

Courageous Hearts: Soul-Nourishing Stories to Inspire You to Embrace Your Fears and Follow Your Dreams (contributor). Compiled by Linda Joy; edited by Bryna René Haynes and Deborah Kevin.

Find links to both at ShamelessMovement.com

Books that continue to inspire me

Joyous Body: Myths and Stories of the Wise Woman Archetype; The Dangerous Old Woman; and *Women Who Run With the Wolves: Myths and Stories of the Wild Woman Archetype* by Clarissa Pinkola Estés

Pussy: A Reclamation and *The School of Womanly Arts* by Regena Thomashauer

Women's Bodies, Women's Wisdom: Creating Physical and Emotional Health and Healing by Christiane Northrup, M.D.

Wild Power: Discover the Magic of Your Menstrual Cycle and Awaken the Feminine Path to Power by Alexandra Pope and Sjanie Hugo Wurlitzer

Keys to the Kingdom and *Understanding Women: Unlock the Mystery* by Alison Armstrong

Witch: Unleashed. Untamed. Unapologetic by Lisa Lister

Sweat your Prayers: The Five Rhythms of the Soul by Gabrielle Roth

Braving the Wilderness: The Quest for True Belonging and the Courage to Stand Alone and *The Gifts of Imperfection: Let Go of Who You Think You're Supposed to Be and Embrace Who You Are* by Brené Brown, Ph.D., L.M.S.W.

Women's Wisdom from the Heart of Africa by Sobonfu Somé

The Body Keeps the Score: Brain, Mind, and Body in the Healing of Trauma by Dr. Bessel Van Der Kolk

Big Magic: Creative Living Beyond Fear by Elizabeth Gilbert

Femalia by Joani Blank

Other resources

TantraNova Institute of Chicago, intimacy programs, Tantric retreats, and bodywork, oh my! Elsbeth Meuth and Freddy Zental are the real deal. Tantranova.com

School of Womanly Arts, courses in radical feminine awakening that's not for the faint of heart. Mamagenas.com

Boldheart, heart-centered business training for purpose-driven spiritualentrepreneurs. Boldheart.com

References

Beck, J. (August 2015). Life's Stories: How you arrange the plot points of your life into a narrative can shape who you are—and is a fundamental part of being human. *The Atlantic*.

https://www.theatlantic.com/health/archive/2015/08/life-stories-narrative-psychology-redemption-mental-health/400796/

Black, M. C., Basile, K. C., Breiding, M. J., Smith, S .G., Walters, M. L., Merrick, M. T., Stevens, M. R. (2011). The National Intimate Partner and Sexual Violence Survey (NISVS): 2010 summary report. http://www.cdc.gov/ViolencePrevention/pdf/NISVS_Report2010-a.pdf

Cuddy, Amy. Presence: Bringing your boldest self to your biggest challenges. Little, Brown & Company (2015).

Gladwell, Malcolm. *Outliers: The story of success*. Little, Brown & Company (2008).

RAINN (Rape, Abuse & Incest National Network) website, https://www.rainn.org/statistics/criminal-justice-system

Rennison, C. M. (2002). Rape and sexual assault: Reporting to police and medical attention, 1992-2000 [NCJ 194530]. Retrieved from the U.S. Department of Justice, Office of Justice Programs, Bureau of Justice Statistics: https://www.bjs.gov/content/pub/pdf/rsarp00.pdf

Smith, S. G., Chen, J., Basile, K. C., Gilbert, L. K., Merrick, M. T., Patel, N., ... Jain, A. (2017). The National Intimate Partner and Sexual Violence Survey (NISVS): 2010-2012 state report. Retrieved from the Centers for Disease Control and Prevention, National Center for Injury Prevention and Control: https://www.cdc.gov/violenceprevention/pdf/NISVS-StateReportBook.pdf

Tucker, Judith Stadtman, “Motherhood, shame and society: An interview with Brené Brown, Ph.D., author of Women & Shame." *The Mothers Movement Online*. http://mothersmovement.org/features/bbrown_int/bbrown_int_1.htm

Acknowledgments

I could not have written this book without the twin centers of my soul, my children, Khai and Thalila Sisou. They have believed in me, unfailingly, from my first tremulous shimmy through my latest book. They see and love me without reserve. My darlings, I could not be prouder of the geniuses you have always been and the leaders you are becoming. I love you so much.

Thank you to my husband, my staunch supporter, Marcin Krzeminski, who believes in me even when I falter and stumble. If I were to say I'm the next Oprah, he'd say, "Sure, Bebeh," without a raised eyebrow or wisp of cynicism. I love you, babe. Thank you for believing in me even when I forget to believe in myself.

To my BFF, my sister by another mister, my platonic wife, my daily grounding goddess, and editor, Kimberly Robb Baker. I am so, so glad to share another lifetime with you. Seriously, this book would not have come to fruition without your encouragement and pushing and faith and did I mention (gentle yet firm) pushing?

To Fabienne Fredrickson and the Boldheart community: Thank you for holding me to the shameless, larger version of myself, always; for surrounding me with unconditional love; and for giving me the occasional, incisive, swift kick in the tush as needed.

To Mama Gena (Regena Thomashauer) and the Sister Goddess tribe of the School of Womanly Arts: thank you for providing tools to access the body's sensual shamelessness and the power of our pleasure, and thank you, above all, for being on-fire, unapologetic representatives of the rising Divine Feminine.

Thank you to the shame and vulnerability researchers whose work makes mine possible, especially Brené Brown, whose own vulnerability, transparency and willingness to take a stand on the most uncomfortable of subjects shows that this woman practices what she preaches, y'all.

Thank you to Rosanne Romiglio, whose divine design graces the cover of this book and is the graphic midwife to my Shameless Movement rebrand. Thank you, soul sister, for nurturing me through my miscarriage. Words cannot convey. So grateful that we are on this journey together.

Thank you to Debbie Kevin for helping to get this book launched into the world, and to all the luscious partners who said YES to sharing it with their tribes. So grateful for your support!

This list would not be complete without the shameless women who led and lead the way, inspiring me to show up every day as all of who I am, including: Maya Angelou, Nina Simone, Dr. Clarissa Pinkola Estes, and so many more gamechangers, suffragettes, and love warriors.

And finally, thank YOU, the brilliant leader who holds my humble offering in your hand. Congratulations on taking this next step to showing up in the world as your whole, brilliant, gorgeous, sexy self. Without apology, without compromise, without shame.
I believe in you. Thank you. I love you.

About the author

Charisse Sisou, Visibility Maven to Women Here to Change the World and Chief Correspondent from Your Happy Place is on a mission: To populate the world with happy women—by empowering those at the leading edge of transformation.

A coach and mentor, she draws from training and experience across industries to conjure her own special kind of magic:

As a speaker and nationally award-winning bellydancer, she's reconnected thousands of women with the hidden reserves of energy, intelligence and healing that reside in every woman's body, speaking in national conferences, online events and podcasts, and women's organizations across the US and beyond.

As a master strategist and communicator, she founded the copy and content agency Claim Your Message, where her team has supported hundreds of executives and entrepreneurs in telling their stories, sharing their gifts, and attracting the clients, community and opportunities they desire. (ClaimYourMessage.com)

And as a former corporate badass and current business owner, she's navigated the challenges we all face as women leaders.

With a BA in Women's Studies from Amherst College and MBA coursework from the Booth School of Business, Charisse is one of those rare teachers equally strategic and creative, analytic and intuitive—

bringing her interdisciplinary approach to the art and science of claiming your feminine power in body, word and business.

Author of *Every Day Pleasure,* contributor to Amazon bestseller *Courageous Hearts*, and founding Queen of *The Shameless Movement*, Charisse leads workshops, retreats and circles with love and a playful heart, inspiring women leaders to DO less and BE more: Show up as ALL of who you are—curves, edges and all.

Charisse works and lives outside Chicago, and dances all over the world. Website: ShamelessMovement.com.